dot-font
talking about design

JOHN D. BERRY

MARK BATTY PUBLISHER

Dot-font: Talking About Design
© 2006 by John D. Berry

DESIGN & PRODUCTION: John D. Berry
TYPEFACES USED: MVB Verdigris (*text*); HTF Whitney (*display and small display*); and Freight (*display on cover*).
COVER IMAGE: Ionesco (*left*) and Massin (*right*), copyright 1965 by Yan (Jean Dieuzaide); droits réservés. Used by permission of Massin.

Photo of Rich Gold (page 27) courtesy of the Palo Alto Research Center, photographed by Deanna Horvath. Photos of "Research in Reading" exhibits (pages 27, 28 & 30) courtesy of Onomy Labs. Photo of 1970 New York City subway map (page 37) courtesy of Massimo Vignelli. Photo of New York subway signage circa 1965 (page 38) copyright New York Transit Museum. Photo of BART signage (page 47) courtesy of EMSEAL floor systems. Museum photographs (page 53, 59 & 60) by Shantel Rodriguez. Images from film footage of Hermann Zapf (page 124) used by permission of Jack Stauffacher.

Library of Congress Control Number:
2006933333

Printed and bound at the National Press
The Hashemite Kingdom of Jordan

10 9 8 7 6 5 4 3 2 1   FIRST EDITION

This edition © 2006
Mark Batty Publisher
36 West 37th Street, Penthouse
New York NY 10018

www.markbattypublisher.com

ISBN-10: 0-9772827-1-6
ISBN-13: 078-09772827-1-5

Contents

DEDICATION
To my partner Eileen Gunn
for continually asking the hardest questions

ACKNOWLEDGMENTS
Thanks to Creativepro (*www.creativepro.com*), for providing the platform on which all of these articles were published, and through which they reached their first audience. In particular, thanks to my editors there: Pamela Pfiffner, Mitt Jones, and Terri Stone. Thanks, too, to Peter Fraterdeus, for graciously letting me use the name "dot-font" without restriction, after having unrealized plans to use it himself. And thanks to all the people I've written about, for doing interesting things.

Thanks to Buzz Poole, Jacob Albert, and Christopher Salyers at Mark Batty Publisher, who all helped to make this book what it is.

Thanks to everybody who supplied images, either for the original columns or for this book — especially to Massin and to Steve Woodall, of the San Francisco Center for the Book, for supplying the cover image. Thanks to Susie Taylor and the San Francisco Public Library, for supplying the footage of Hermann Zapf and Jack Stauffacher in 1960, and to Axel Roesler of the University of Washington, for capturing still images from that footage.

Thanks to Mark van Bronkhorst, Jonathan Hoefler, and Josh Darden, for the use of their fonts, respectively: MVB Verdigris (text), HTF Whitney (display), and Freight (cover display).

introduction | John D. Berry

"Dot-font" is the running title of the column I've been writing for the past half-dozen years for *Creativepro .com*, an online portal aimed at creative professionals. The column is part of an ongoing conversation with the design field. Its focus has been on typography and design, though as you can imagine the subject matter has ranged far afield at times. In a companion volume to this small book (*Dot-font: Talking About Fonts*), I've collected some of the essays with a particular focus on type; in this book, by contrast, I've gathered essays about design in general, or about particular aspects of it. But type is never far from the surface; there's very little in graphic design that doesn't involve type and lettering in some form, and the written language is embedded in almost every aspect of our daily lives.

I've never been very interested in observing boundaries anyway; it's usually at the edges, where definitions blur, that things get most interesting.

The articles that I've chosen to reprint here follow a natural flow within each section, but it's not always a chronological one. For that reason, I've given the date of original publication at the beginning of each column; sometimes the context requires it. In its original form, on an active website, each article included a multitude of links — to people or books or sites referred to, sometimes to related ideas, and of course to sources or background information on fonts. There's no point to including such links in a printed book; you could find them more easily, and in more up-to-date form, by Googling the key words. In a handful of places, I've included a Web address (after first checking to make sure that, at least as I write this, the link is still live) where the website was the particular focus of what I was writing about. Otherwise, you're on your own.

Design is an amorphous subject, and an ambiguous but highly useful profession. The purpose of design is to give clarity and form to the shapelessness of everyday life — or at least to create some structures that help us navigate within the everyday chaos. Maybe that's why it's so hard to pin down any particular definition of "design." Plenty of designers and non-designers have promulgated theories and manifestoes, but what matters is their practice. One of the reasons I started writing "dot-font" is that we all live in the midst of design every hour of the day; at the beginning of the 21st century, we live in a designed world, for better or worse. We might as well pay attention to it, and turn an observant and critical eye on what's around us.

practice & ideas

Massin:
the unclassifiable free thinker

The innovative graphic work of Massin exhibited in the United States, in a show that inspires and frees up designers.

[*June 27, 2003*]

The severe shapes of the characters in THE BALD SOPRANO *turn the blank page into a stage.*

THE FRENCH GRAPHIC DESIGNER Massin is best known in this country for his ground-breaking typographic and visual treatment of the Eugene Ionesco play *The Bald Soprano* (*La Cantatrice chauve*), first published in France by Gallimard in 1964. Massin's interpretation of Ionesco's absurdist play was groundbreaking: using a playful collage of posterized black-and-white photographs of the actors in silhouette, surrounded by sprays and cascades of type in varying sizes and styles (without benefit of cartoonish effects like word balloons), he created a juxtaposition of type and image in book form that became a classic of expressive typography. The stark images from *The Bald Soprano* are instantly recognizable — both the characters and their jumbled words.

But Massin has done a great deal more than just this one notable book. The exhibition "Massin in Continuo: A Dictionary," which originated at Cooper Union in New York and toured to Los Angeles, Boston, Baltimore, and Minneapolis before coming to San Francisco, explores Massin's long career as a book designer, typographer, art director, writer, photographer, and music aficionado. An abridged "dictionary" ran over the summer of 2003 at the San Francisco Center for the Book. The abridgement was necessary, says SFCB artistic director Steve Woodall, because of the Center's limited exhibit space, but it presented an opportunity to focus on "what is arguably Massin's most interesting work: his early projects with Club du Meilleur Livre and his influential typographic experiments of the 1960s."

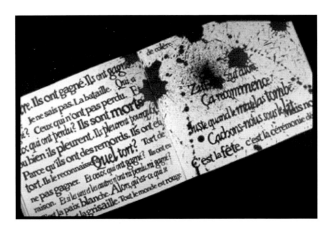

Education of a Renaissance man

Massin started early. At the age of seven, he was producing small books that he would both write and lay out,
signing them "Robert Massin, Author, Editor, Publisher,
Typographer, and Photographer." As a child, he absorbed
all the graphic images and letter forms to be found in his
grandmother's grocery shop: logos, packaging, signs,
posters, and enamel advertising plaques. He was a vora-
cious consumer of vernacular culture. Even earlier, when
he was only four, his father (a stone engraver) gave him
a hammer and chisel and asked him to engrave his name
in soft stone — even though the young Massin did not
yet know how to write the alphabet. "This remains in my
imagination a founding moment of my interest in letters
and all graphic things," he says. The exposure to letters
as images in their own right as well as carriers of meaning set the stage for Massin's lifelong career of graphic
experimentation.

Designing books

He began designing books in 1949 for the Club du Meilleur Livre, one of the major book clubs that flourished
in France after the Second World War, in a time when
there was no functioning network of bookstores across

Type used expressively for the cover of BOURLINGUER, *by Blaise Cendrars (Club du Meilleur Livre, 1953).*

Cover (back, front, and spine) of L'OR *by Blaise Cendrars, designed for the Club du Meilleur Livre in 1954.*

the country. For several years, the book clubs were the principal means of publishing and distributing literature in France, and the designers and art director had a free hand in presenting their texts. Massin credits his mentor Pierre Faucheux with inspiring his own approach to the books. "Faucheux had been one of the first designer/ typographers to emphasize the importance of dynamic typography and documentary iconography on covers, at a time when illustration had not yet been replaced by photography. For my first covers, I was asking myself, 'What would Pierre Faucheux think?'" Massin describes himself and his fellow (sometimes competing) book-club art directors as "graphic acrobats."

From an early date, Massin was influenced not only by the traditions of book design but by the innovations of film: Saul Bass's title sequences for the movies of Alfred Hitchcock, and Tex Avery's animated cartoons. "I have spoken often," he says, "about the cinematic quality of book design, revealing its narrative structure while constantly changing scale and rhythm, and alternating focal planes and perspective. Between the endpapers and the first signature, it was like creating a little flip-book within the book. It was quite common to have these elaborate introductory pages in the Clubs' books."

Massin finds inspiration in popular culture, and as a book designer, he puts these influences to work in interpreting the text. In the words of the exhibition's curator, Laetitia Wolff, "While an innovator in typography, he has shown respect for classic, romantic, and popular art, integrating graphic elements of other epochs to match the content and context of a book he is designing." For Blaise Cendrars's *L'Or* (*Gold*, Club du Meilleur Livre, 1954), for example, Massin cut out letters from an 1848 American poster and used them to match the visual style of the California Gold Rush.

Eugene Ionesco (left) and Massin with the original French edition of LA CANTATRICE CHAUVE.

Book series

For the publisher Gallimard, whom he worked for as an art director for twenty years, Massin created the "Folio" line of popular literary paperbacks in 1972. He had to design 300 layouts in less than six months to launch the new line. Since the bright white Kromekote paper stock had recently been introduced by Champion Paper, he gave all the books a recognizable identity with bright white backgrounds, and used a consistent typeface, Baskerville Old Style, juxtaposed against unique illustrations. It was an uphill battle to convince the sales force that the pocket books they were selling were meant to be kept, not just read once and thrown away. They were a long-term success. The Folio paperbacks can still be easily found in any French bookstore, although today their cover images are more likely to be stock photos than the original illustrations that Massin commissioned from notable illustrators such as Folon, Ronald Searle, and Roland Topor. (Massin still has a few of the original drawings framed on his walls.)

Each character speaks in his or her own typeface.

All the world's a page

Massin went to twenty different performances of *La Cantatrice Chauve* at the Théâtre de la Huchette in Paris. He even recorded the play so he could catch the inflections, intonations, and pauses of the actors as they spoke, and then transform them into an interplay of photographs and type. Ionesco's play deals with breaking down clichés and thoughtless truisms into absurd caricature; it has been described as an anti-play. Massin's treatment on the page reflected that disjointedness and conveyed it graphically. He gave each character a different typeface, varying the size, angle, and placement to convey the nuances of the spoken dialogue.

"Massin's version," says Wolff, "created with the blessings of Ionesco, sought to capture the dynamism of the theatre within the static confines of the book." Massin himself says that he "introduced the notion of stage time and space to the printed page."

Still bending expectations
Massin has designed and art-directed many other books and lines of books over the years, as well as writing several. His own books have included *Letter & Image* (*La Lettre et L'Image*, Gallimard, 1970), a comprehensive study of the interaction of letters and images through human history, and a theoretical treatise on page layout, *La Mise en Page* (Hoëbeke, 1991), which he both wrote and designed.

The techniques he uses to create his expressive kind of typography have changed with changing technology; today he works with digital publishing tools like Photoshop and Illustrator. *The Bald Soprano* had to be created in painstaking physical paste-ups on boards; he didn't even have the advantage of phototype, which was not in common use yet in the early 1960s. One technique he used in order to freely change the shapes of letters, in the days before computer type, was to have them printed on condoms, which he then pinned down in stretched and distorted form and photographed.

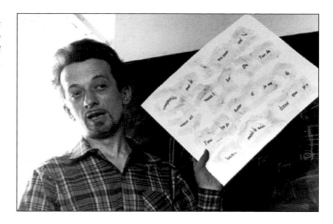

As Laetitia Wolff concludes in her introduction of
Massin and his work, "This free-spirited and compulsive
creator is the unsung hero of an immense graphic heri-
tage. Make way for Massin."

Rick Poynor's vices & virtues

Former *Eye* editor Rick Poynor issues a call for critical thinking among graphic designers.

[*May 25, 2001*]

Rick Poynor's 2001 collection of essays on design

RICK POYNOR, design critic and founder of the incisive British graphic-design magazine *Eye*, spoke to an audience of graphic designers in San Francisco in May 2001, as part of the Design Lecture Series sponsored by the local AIGA and SFMOMA. He presented his audience, which looked to be mostly young designers, with a sort of "manifesto" (he made the quotes audible) about graphic design, consisting largely of paired lists of "six vices" and "six virtues." It was a call to responsibility and intelligence, and a cry against the complacency of uncritical thinking. Judging from the few questions and remarks from the audience at the end, I'm not sure whether his thoughtful seeds fell on fertile ground.

Editor & design critic Rick Poynor

Manifestoes then & now
Poynor has very solid credentials, as well as a track record of critical writing in the graphic-design field. I've always

First Things First 2000

found his way of presenting his ideas just a little too academic for my taste — just a little too much of the jargon of academe, even though he often turns it on itself for his own purposes — but perhaps by using that language he can reach out to people immured in the academic fortress and seduce them into noticing the rest of the world. (Yes, of course I exaggerate — but we all know the tendencies that infest the academic world and that undermine its strengths. Goading and gadflying are constantly required.)

The overblown promotional copy about Poynor in the program (which of course he can hardly be held responsible for) calls him "the messiah of message over medium." It goes on, "In a recent manifesto, he argued that designers need to worry about meaning more than marketing, and content instead of branding." The manifesto referred to is *First Things First 2000*, which Poynor helped organize, the updated version of a rallying call first issued by 22 "visual communicators" in 1964. Both the original and the renewed version (33 signers in 1999) are clear attacks on commercialism, urging graphic designers to put usefulness and concern for the public weal ahead of their pocketbooks — or at least to avoid confusing the two.

In a way, Poynor's talk was an elaboration of this idea. After all, as he pointed out, the uncritical blending of salesmanship and culture is the condition of our times. We could use some clear-eyed discrimination of one thing from another — both when there seemed to be an unending wave of esteem and money that graphic designers could ride forever, and now when the wave has crashed and everyone is trying to turn life rafts into surfboards and escape the wreckage.

The Vices
Poynor's six vices are:
1. *Relativism*
2. *Commerce = culture*

3. *Noise*

4. *Homogeneity*

5. *Rebellion*

6. *The Blockbuster effect*

By *relativism*, he means the widespread assumption that everyone's opinion is just as "valid" as everyone else's, so that no value judgments are possible. He quoted an "American phrase" that he said seemed to be making great inroads in this country (I confess I hadn't heard it before): "It's all good." As you might guess, Poynor doesn't believe for a moment that every opinion is as good as the last. Open-mindedness, yes; flaccid thinking and a refusal to take stands, no.

This question poses itself in the context of our current society, which seems based on the assumption that *commerce* and *culture* are the same thing. How often have we heard our culture described purely in terms of what sells, what's popular, what the divine Market has decided to value? Poynor spent quite a while on this subject, pointing to the confusion between editorial content and marketing in such "magalogs" as *Sony Style*, which sell a consumer lifestyle as a way of life. Where, he asked, is the independent point of view that we expect to find in real art, when it has been subsumed into a marketing tool?

The distinction of an "independent point of view" is a very important one. At the end of the talk, one of the audience members asked Poynor how he would deal with the inherent conflict in getting corporate sponsorship for expensive events like this series of design lectures. Poynor acknowledged that it's always a question, and that, in essence, eternal vigilance is necessary, but he also pointed out that, while he wasn't familiar with the sponsors of his own talk, no one had tried to dictate an agenda to him or censor him in any way. At times, the influence of sponsors can be benign. The possibility for corruption (intellectual as well as monetary) is always there, but that doesn't mean it's always indulged.

"Anti-design"? A poster by Mevis and Van Deusen

By *noise*, Poynor meant simply the distractions and diversions of our "information society"—where so much of the so-called information inundating us is just noise.

Poynor's fourth vice, *homogeneity*, doesn't strike me as such a vicious problem. Perhaps in Europe it really is possible to feel that the agenda of "good design" has been carried out to such a degree that there's truly "too much design" in the everyday world, but that's not part of my daily experience of living in the United States. Poynor has a declared preference for the uncertain, the unfinished, the rough-edged over the slick, and he quite rightly heaps scorn on graphic design that looks clean and sharp and finely made but says nothing. But there's nothing about clean design that implies superficiality, and nothing about rough "non-design" that implies authenticity.

Poynor touched on this with his fifth vice, *rebellion*. He was acknowledging something that's been happening since the end of the 1960s, when rebellion informed a whole segment of our culture: the "co-opting" (to use the 1970s term) of protest and rebellion into the mainstream. Thirty years ago, jeans companies were using images of the counterculture to market their product to the very people who saw themselves as rebels; today, fonts and graphic styles created as an anti-design statement are being used to sell us everything from cold remedies to cars.

The *Blockbuster effect* is nothing more than the commercial enforcement of homogeneity by huge chain stores in every neighborhood with identical, unvarying product lines. He used the Blockbuster chain of video stores as his example. (His local outlet looks just the same as one in Chattanooga or one in San Francisco. The ones in the TV commercials are the best—patronized solely by fashion models with luxurious apartments, and suffused with an ethereal glow. "My local store lacks this last feature," he said.)

The virtues

So what are the six virtues with which Poynor would counter these sins?

1. *Being critical*
2. *History*
3. *Smallness*
4. *Imperfection*
5. *Responsibility*
6. *Refusal*

Perhaps these are self-explanatory. Turning a *critical* eye on the world around us, including its graphic design, seems an obvious response to living in a world that's trying to sell us something all the time. And if criticism is going to be anything more than reflexive rebellion, we have to know something of what came before this moment: therefore, *history*. (Poynor didn't point out that there's nothing more fascinating than finding out what went before, the campfire tales that make up history. It's not all academic jargon and exam questions.)

Smallness is a reaction to the all-blanketing chains as well as to the megabuck theory that only what's big and appeals to a mass audience is important. (Curiously, he said, people who advocate paying attention to a smaller audience are frequently dismissed as "elitist." What could be more effectively, indeed efficiently, elitist than the tyranny of the huge?) His "smallness" could also be described as "localness," since it's the local, "site-specific" things that Poynor cherishes. He cited the example of Cornel Windlin, a Swiss designer in his mid-thirties who worked in London for several years and then returned to Zurich, where he makes posters and other graphic works that are tied to local events. Windlin also worries that perhaps he's too isolated or limited in Zurich, away from the metropolis, from London or New York. Poynor suggests that while these worries are natural enough, perhaps they aren't all that important.

I've already alluded to Poynor's preference for the *imperfect*, the unpolished, the rough-hewn. He quoted Robert Venturi's phrase "messy vitality," and argued that since design is something fundamental to being human, it can't be left solely in the hands of designated practitioners. Poynor seemed to think that design professionals had taken the possibility of designing things away from the public through increasing professionalization. To me that seems like a perspective that's only possible from inside the design profession; in the real world, I'd say that graphic design is practiced by far more people today than ever before. As a designer, I'm always trying to instill a higher level of excellence in the design that's produced, but I'm very, very happy to see the tools of design in so many hands.

Responsibility should be obvious by now. Designers, like any other citizens of our world, have to take responsibility for their effect on everyone else; neither graphic design nor any other profession exists in a vacuum. As Poynor pointed out, graphic designers claim great importance for their work, right up to the point where someone asks them to take responsibility for the effect of what they do. "We can't have it both ways," he said. The counter to this is *refusal* — the refusal to take on morally odious work, but also the refusal to live our whole lives as consumers. He cited the extreme example of Michael Landy, an artist in London who set up a storefront art project on Oxford Street where a team of workmen fed all of his belongings into an industrial machine that turned them into recyclable grains. Poynor didn't suggest that anyone else ought to do this (he wasn't about to himself), but he held it up as a fine gesture. Responding to a question from the audience, he said that the interesting thing might be to interview Landy a year later and find out whether he'd replaced all the material goods he tossed away.

The audience

Poynor was certainly speaking to the right audience. Who could embody more precisely the group of people his questions are directed at than an AIGA crowd attending a Design Lecture across the street from the San Francisco Museum of Modern Art? Judging from the questions at the end, his vice of relativism is alive and well, and the habit of critical thinking isn't practiced among designers as carefully as one might wish. I was surprised by his saying that he thought the kind of discussion embodied by this lecture series was seldom found in design talks in the UK (where I think of the art of intelligent criticism as being more developed than here; perhaps it's just a facility with debating techniques), but I was encouraged by the large audience. Maybe some of them will go home and find themselves arguing with him.

Boundary disorders

When are designers out of bounds?

[June 29, 2001]

AT THE OPENING of the TDC47 and TDC² 2001 exhibition in New York City, designer/educator Carol Winer introduced a wonderful term to the world of type and design: "boundary disorders." (Or perhaps this phrase has been part of her vocabulary for a long time; it was new to me, and it appeared to be new to everyone who heard it.) She suggested this as a descriptive name for a sort of disjunction and disconnection that afflicts many people and situations in the new century — especially designers.

The idea grew out of a conversation about spelling, of all things. Someone observed that people who grow up on computers with spelling checkers often don't know how to spell, "and don't have to." (The same has been said about the arithmetical skills of people raised on calculators.) Although I said I thought the ability to spell correctly in our arduous and arbitrary language was probably a talent found in the same proportion in any generation, it's certainly true that there's a difference between having to rely entirely on your memory (or looking in a reference book) and having software handle much of the task for you as you work.

Personal space

Carol suggested that the kinds of technology we all use break down many of the boundaries we set up and negotiate in our daily lives. In a sense, technology is all about breaking boundaries (geographic, productivity, etc.), but it doesn't take many dinner-hour sales calls to figure out that not all boundary crossing is positive.

The boundaries we used to take for granted, such as geographical boundaries, are routinely crossed these days. In a literal sense, people and ideas cross borders more freely today than ever (despite the best efforts of many governing bodies to prevent it). And technology has leapfrogged physical boundaries in so many ways that we're quite used to feeling "closer" to someone thousands of miles away than to the people right next door. But in many ways our day-to-day expectations are still based on habits acquired through millennia of face-to-face communication.

"Have you ever been at a party," Carol Winer said, "where someone is looking toward you and talking, but you realize they're really speaking to a little microphone on their lapel?"

This reflects a confusion of personal boundaries. In any social interaction, we usually expect the lines of communication to have some clear physical relation to the closeness of actual human beings. If you think someone at a party is talking to you and it turns out they're not, you'd expect to find the person they're really talking to right behind you or next to you — not someplace else entirely. But these expectations can't really be taken for granted anymore. As we carry more and more modes of communication and information retrieval on our bodies in daily life, we may need wholly different notions of what a boundary is and where it lies.

Work & play

How does this relate to designers? you ask.

That's easy. Haven't you ever been working on a project at long distance and spent a fortune on Fed Ex packages back and forth? And don't you find that these days you're saving on the Fed Ex bills but you're getting last-minute changes from clients by e-mail at any hour of the day or night? (Someone else at the TDC opening was heard to declare, tongue not entirely in cheek, "E-mail is evil!")

Designers deal with boundary disorders on a daily basis. Since clients can reach us nearly any time and any place, people tend to expect a quicker turnaround. The boundaries between the "work day" and the rest of the day — or the rest of the week, or the rest of life — have mostly dissolved for anyone working in the creative high-tech field. We all recognize this (otherwise why would we laugh so loud at *Dilbert*?), but we may not think about what new kinds of boundaries are being set up — and violated.

How does the traditional boundary of the "deadline" change in this fluid environment? Does telecommuting, for instance, or working as a freelancer from afar make it easier to miss or push deadlines? Or does it simply reduce the elapsed time to smaller and smaller increments? Maybe some boundaries are better left unbroken.

Not to get too self-referential here, but... My own frequent editor on this column, Creativepro's Mitt Jones, is someone I've worked with for most of a year, exchanging e-mail and occasional phone calls, though we're in entirely different cities and have never met. Commenting on an earlier draft of this column, he said, "I'm thinking of how we work with people from a distance electronically, often without ever having met them, and I wonder how this affects boundaries. When people deal with one another in person, they tacitly negotiate some types of boundaries, don't they — interpersonal boundaries. I guess we do the same thing electronically, but the boundaries are a different set of boundaries, pertaining to a different communication medium."

How much do boundaries change over time?

No end in sight
This is an amorphous subject, because we're all new at this game. I have no answers for it, just questions.

Our world changes too fast to rely entirely on tradition for guidance, yet we can't exist in a state of constant uncertainty and anxiety. Perhaps all we can do is keep paying attention to the boundaries around us — both the ones we run up against and the ones we set up — and keep asking ourselves again and again which ones are useful, which ones are needlessly restrictive.

At the exhibition opening, Carol Winer and I had been talking about initiating a series of small talks and forums sponsored by the TDC, and Carol offered this notion of boundary disorders as a starting point for a possibly lively discussion among designers. It might turn out to be the starting point for a never-ending re-examination of our whole way of life.

Reading into the future

Xerox PARC's forward-looking Rich Gold turned ideas about reading inside out. Before his early death in 2002, he talked about the future of reading — and about the task of authoring text in a digital world.

[*August 10, 2001*]

Rich Gold

RICH GOLD LIKES to turn expectations on their heads. And he gets paid to do it. In fact, he gets to run an entire department devoted to what he calls, alternately, "speculative engineering" and "speculative design."

At the recent Book Tech West conference in San Francisco, Gold was one of two keynote speakers. Since Book Tech chose, oddly, to schedule the two separate keynote speeches against each other, I can't tell you anything about the other (by Adobe's e-book guy Kevin Nathanson), but of all the talks and presentations I heard, Gold's was hands-down the most energetic and fascinating. Clearly, Gold takes delight in tossing out ideas; his lively patter was full of them.

The Reading Wall

The future of reading

Rich Gold is the head of a multidisciplinary laboratory, called RED, or "Research in Experimental Documents," at Xerox PARC. The subject of his talk was "The Future of Reading," and RED has addressed this question in a number of unusual ways. The most highly visible is its exhibit last year at the Tech Museum in San Jose, "Experiments in the Future of Reading," which is currently on tour around the country. The San Jose exhibit featured such

Scenes from the future of reading?

things as Very Long Books (physical walls o' book), Very Fast Books (quick!—what was that word?), Deep Books (books you can "drill into"), and even Sensitive Books (tackling how people think and feel about different writing systems from around the world).

Despite repeated assertions of how boring everyone thinks his subject is ("Reading? Yawn"), Gold repeatedly made startling statements about what reading is and how we do it. First he pointed out that our mental image of a solitary individual sitting in a chair with a good book is just one aspect of reading—and not the way most reading is actually done. Reading is all around us; it's in the air, sometimes quite literally, with wayfinding, signage, advertising, and even portable language—the stuff we wear on our own bodies. Reading defines where we are in the physical world.

Gold said humans have both bibliographic cultures and epigraphic cultures: cultures that read in books or similar compendiums of words, in private, and cultures that read publicly displayed words. (I suspect it's a bit facile to call these separate cultures, since in our own culture we do both all the time. But recognizing the distinction is useful.) Bibliographic reading is mostly done on a horizontal surface, like a library table or a lap; epigraphic reading is done from a vertical surface, like the side of a building. Museums, he pointed out, are essentially "large epigraphic reading experiences."

He also delved into how much we can modulate the media we use to communicate: not just surfaces covered with writing but the air around us (when we speak, making sound waves), or pieces of paper (once we've written on it, we can't easily unwrite our words), or computer screens.

Authoring all the way down
Gold showed a little matrix he uses to categorize the areas his group works in: Art, Science, Design, and

Art	Science
Design	Engineering

Rich Gold's matrix of the areas that RED's *work falls into*

Engineering. He drew a square with four compartments; the top two were Art (left) and Science (right), while the bottom two were Design (left) and Engineering (right). He said there was a fundamental difference between the areas above and below the center line — a functional difference based on who the people engaged in each of those areas have to deal with most often. Those who work in Art and Science have to satisfy Patrons and Peers; those who work in Design and Engineering are more dependent on Customers and Users.

He used the term "authoring" a lot, and he questioned the idea of simple passive reading. As a practical matter, the company Gold works for, Xerox, is interested in producing "a book a minute" and getting that book into the hands of the people who want it. In the expected coming age of "ubiquitous computing," when there may be no such thing as a separate "computer" but computational power is built in to almost every manmade object (like the three or four "computers" found in any automobile today), the distinctions we make now between e-books and print-on-demand volumes may simply not matter. Gold talked about what he called "total writing: authoring all the way down": instead of making up pure text and sending it out in the world to be treated or mistreated at will, the creator manipulates everything about the way that text is received, from the design of the page to, conceivably, the environment in which it's read. To complement this, he spoke of "deep reading." ("We should have called it 'total reading,' but it turned out that someone already had the phrase trademarked.")

Gold is skeptical of the currently popular idea of "convergent" reading or publishing. The symbol of this is the e-book, where any piece of text can be downloaded to the same reading device — the same medium — and be treated the same. Gold described one of his favorite books when he was a child, a book about elephants where the pages were actually cut into the shape of an elephant, so that the book itself was (when held or seen from the side) a little elephant. "You can't put the elephant book in an e-book," said Gold.

"Image, genre, media, and context are all authorable," he said. This is what he meant by "authoring all the way down." If he's right, it's a golden opportunity for people who can combine disciplines and work not only with "content" but with everything about the *context* of that content — with pretty much everything, in fact, within reach.

Rich Gold with the "tilty table," or Very Wide Book.

How we'll read

Rich Gold's talk was the sort that makes you walk out with your head spinning. I know I, for one, could spend a lot more of my time in what he calls "speculative design." The future of reading will include everything that's gone before, but it's going to include a lot we can't even dream of yet. What better than to spend your days pushing the frontiers of the dream?

OK to typeset

What's the process of how type really gets set today? And where does the line fall between editorial and design?

[*November 18, 2002*]

REMEMBER WHEN writing a document and typesetting it were two entirely different things, separate processes performed by different people at different times? No?

Well, back in ancient days—the late 20th century—there was a pragmatic separation between creating what we now call "content" and formatting it visually for presentation to its audience. The first part—creation of the words—would be done on a typewriter, or on a piece of paper by hand, or later on a word-processor; the second part would be done on a large, complex, expensive proprietary typesetting system, at first in hot metal and later in film or early digital type. The skills involved in design and production were not necessarily those needed for writing and editing.

To be sure, sometimes there was close collaboration; there had to be, to make things come out right. In advertising agencies, especially, there would often be an intense back-and-forth between copywriter and designer. But neither the designer nor the writer was the typesetter; ultimately, the ad copy had to be sent out to a type house to be set in type, which would then be pasted up by hand.

When paper was king, you had to rubber-stamp the printed copy to show whether it was approved and ready to go into production.

Type without direction
Today, when everything is written, designed, and typeset on a Mac or a PC, there are very few type houses left, and the professional typesetter is often dishonored and

When paper was king, you had to rubber-stamp the printed copy to show whether it was approved and ready to go into production.

forgotten. Most typesetting is done in-house, where it's left to the designers or their assistants. But most graphic designers never get more than rudimentary training in typography; they never learn the painstaking craft of making words on a page read effortlessly and well.

Once, it was common in large companies and ad agencies to have a "type director," someone who knew the ins and outs of type and how to get it to look right. The type director wasn't the typesetter; he (more rarely, she) would be in charge of setting standards of typography, and making sure that the type was spec'd right and that what came back from the type house was acceptable. The type director oversaw the typographic identity of everything that went out of the agency or the company.

The position of "type director" largely disappeared when desktop publishing took over, but ironically it's a skill more needed today than ever. All these companies that produce their own type could use someone whose job it is to pay attention to type standards. A glance at a page of almost any popular magazine these days makes this obvious.

Between editing and design
With the words flowing back and forth between "content" and "design," there's a blurring today between design considerations and editorial decisions. Copyeditors and proofreaders often find themselves making judgment calls on things that are rightly part of the typographic design, such as how many lines in a row may end with a hyphen.

When I worked at Microsoft Press in its early days, we had two proofreading departments: editorial proofreaders and production proofreaders. The editorial proofreaders were responsible for checking to see that the words were right; the production proofreaders were responsible for checking to see that the words were typeset right.

When "OK to typeset" was stamped on the copy, it was ready to leave the editorial department.

When, as part of a reorganization in the mid-1980s, one of the proofreading departments was dropped as redundant, things began to fall through the cracks. One chapter of a book suffered an unusual typesetting error: the small-caps command had been turned on at the beginning of the chapter, but inadvertently never turned off, and the whole chapter went through production typeset in small caps. Only when the galleys were sent to the editor did anyone notice. (Unfortunately, galleys were sent out at the same time to the author, who was understandably disconcerted.)

Somewhat later, at a busy type house in Seattle, I observed how the production proofreader could become the arbiter of typographic style. This shop was so busy that it had round-the-clock shifts. A lot of the business was advertising, which saw frequent changes and revisions, often being sent back later in the day by the client. Turnaround was so fast that in these cases an ad might be worked on at different times by different typesetters working on different shifts; the proofreader, working the day shift, would try to keep the typographic details consistent, even to the point of marking changes to the kerning. This infuriated some of the nighttime typesetters, who might come back to find their careful kerning changed; but it was the result of dedication and attention to detail on everyone's part. These conflicts were inevitable when a complex job was being done, on an impossible schedule, by a conflagration of perfectionists. (If you have a better collective noun for perfectionists, please let me know.)

Flexible precision

In practical terms, today, what's needed is more care and attention to detail but less rigidity. Rules (such as that old bugaboo about hyphen stacks) are just guidelines, reflections of patterns; they should be used as such, rather than applied blindly. There's no virtue in following rules;

the rules exist solely to help us create a good result. Whoever is setting our type needs to have a good knowledge of those patterns and why they exist; it should not be up to the editor or the proofreader to plug the gap and make decisions about how the words should be typeset. Perhaps more training in typography for both editors and graphic designers would help — to increase each one's understanding of what the other does.

real-world effects

Underground typography

A journey through the bowels of our transit systems in search of enlightenment and a few clear directions.
[*March 23, 2001*]

THERE ARE FEW more obviously functional forms of environmental typography than the signage in a subway or other transit system. A couple of years ago, I found myself riding the subways of New York, London, and Paris, all in the space of the same month. This gave me an unusual opportunity to compare the three systems first-hand, and to judge which was easiest to navigate.

All three cities have had subways for a long time, so their subway systems have become conglomerations of once-independent underground rail lines, and palimp-sests of various systems of naming, numbering, and signage imposed over the decades. The hodgepodge nature of the subways makes their signage all the more important.

From end to end in Paris
The Paris Métro is the simplest, conceptually. Each line just runs from one end to the other, without branching off into multiple directions (usually), and each is identi-fied by the name of the station on either end. The trouble is that several of the lines have been extended since I first learned the system many years ago, and they are conse-quently identified by the names of the new stations that now terminate the lines. Luckily, each line is also num-bered, and the numbers seem to be given more promi-nence since the expansion than they used to be.

The signage typefaces vary, but quite a lot of the signs are in a face designed for the purpose by Adrian Frutiger (creator of Univers and the eponymous type family Frutiger), which serves admirably. More recently, Jean-François Porchez developed a new typeface for Métro

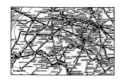

Paris Métro maps: several years ago (top) and recent (second from top); London Underground map (third from top) and the 1970 New York City subway map

signage — one that also works well. Finding the correct train is generally easy, even in a complicated station — even, in fact, where construction has made it necessary to direct riders who are changing lines outside the station itself, across a square, and through parts of a large train station in order to reach the connecting subway line. But it's not always easy, when you're on a train, to spot the name of the station as you pull in.

Knowing where you are in London
The London Underground is famous for its bold, clear station signs, with the easy-to-spot logo of circle and red bar, and for its completely stylized, nearly abstract system map — the first of its kind when it came out early in the last century. The map tells you nothing about the land over your head, but it provides a perfectly understandable schematic of the system itself. (It cannot, however, do much to warn you about the vast distances between "connecting" lines in complex tangles like Paddington Station. The signs directing you through that major rail terminus to the various Underground lines are numerous but misleading.)

What struck me most about the London system, however, was that on every train I rode, it was always possible to see (unless someone was standing in my way) the name of the station clearly displayed outside the window on either side. Not only are there signs at very frequent intervals along the platforms, but there are signs all along the wall on the far side of the tracks, too — and they align perfectly with the windows of the cars. For clarity and, most of all, consistency, London wins hands down.

Local knowledge in New York City
The New York subway system, as you might guess, is the most chaotic as well as the most complex. It's really not right to call it a "system"; it is many systems, laid on top of each other over the years, and many, many exceptions.

The cacophony of New York subway signage, circa 1965

(It's sort of like the English language, where the exceptions seem to outnumber the rules.) When I moved back there three years ago, it took me months of frustration before I remembered what I'd forgotten: that New Yorkers take great pride and perverse delight in mastering the intricacies of their subways, like inhabitants of a great forest knowing how to find the watering-hole where the bears like to gather. The lines have all been numbered or lettered, and color-coded, for more than thirty years, but you still hear people referring blithely to the "East Side IRT" or the "Lexington Avenue Local."

New York subway lines are now designated with single letters or numbers. The signage uses a version of Akzidenz Grotesk, a precursor to Helvetica.

When I first started riding the New York subways, in the late '60s, this system had just been instituted in an attempt to impose a rational overlay on the organic chaos of daily travel. As I learned much later, it was Massimo Vignelli and his design office who gave Gotham a new, consistent system, and he took the idea behind the London Underground map one step farther, in creating the now-famous wiring-diagram map of New York's vastly complicated subway lines. (Today's map is a compromise — equally complex, but much more organic.)

It was a marvelous conceptual map, and it was easy to read. It was a tool for navigating the subways, although not one for navigating the city streets; you had to know where you were going. (Only recently did I find out that Vignelli had planned a second, complementary map that would have been more tied to the actual above-ground geography. The city never let him do it.) There were landmarks that I knew only as subway stations, where I changed trains deep underground without ever knowing what the streets and buildings above me looked like. But it was easy to navigate within the system itself.

The one exception was one I ran afoul of when I was first learning my way around, and it was the result, I assume, of the time it takes to actually implement any ambitious system of re-labeling an entire city. The new maps identified the lines solely by their letters or numbers, not by the names of the three formerly separate transit companies that had been united (the IRT, the BMT, and the IND). But in stations where lines from two or more of the old companies crossed, the actual signs you'd see embedded in the tile walls often said "IRT Uptown" or "This Way to BMT Trains." It was a while before the colorful new circles with their identifying numbers or letters were installed in all the hundreds of stations.

That's not a problem now. With all the Vignelli-inspired signs in their bold, '60s-looking sans serif (a version of Akzidenz Grotesk, the precursor of Helvetica), there's a consistency to much of the signage in New York's underground. But the walls are still full of much older signs — tiles and carved plaster and plaques with curlicues — as well as some more recent attempts at updating the system that don't work particularly well. These signs, old and new, appear at all sorts of different heights and positions, and the various kinds of subway cars all seem to have different windows on varying levels, with plenty of posts and sign-holders blocking the view in inconsistent ways. All this adds up to a situation where often you can't look out the train window and tell what station you're in. (During rush hour, when I was jammed in among a crush of fellow commuters and could only see a small patch of station platform between the arms, legs, and newspapers, I learned to recognize prominent stations by the patterns of construction in their walls. "Oh, it's Fourteenth Street. Three more stops.")

The walls of some stations in the New York subway system still direct riders to the long-merged IRT, BMT, or IND lines.

The most counter-productive contribution to this signage mess is what appears to be an attempt to save on materials and installation costs by putting the name of the station only on every other one of the pillars that march down many station platforms, rather than on each pillar. This is not very useful if your car stops in front of one of the unlabeled pillars. In addition, the newer signs are only found on the front and back sides of the pillars, as though subway riders were suburban commuters facing forward or back in their seats; the old, tiled signs, with their peculiar abbreviations so that long names could fit ("BL'KER" for Bleeker), at least appear on all four sides of the pillars, so they can be read from any direction.

In the New York subway system, old and new styles of signage exist side by side.

Audiovisual aids

When the station signage is inadequate, you have to rely on getting your information inside the car itself.

The last time I was in New York, I got to ride one of the brand-new cars, designed by Antenna Design, which had been getting a lot of notice in the design press. (Only a few were on the tracks at that point.) In practice, when they pull up to a station platform and you get on, they don't seem all that radically different from the old "Redbird" cars (which, according to press reports, may soon find their decommissioned carcasses lying full fathom five off the New Jersey and Long Island coasts, as "artificial reefs" to attract fish). The new cars seem practical and unusually pleasant, but ultimately they're just a new style, not a wildly different approach to riding the subway. They've got the same old ads for Dr. Z's skin-care treatments.

But they do have, unlike anything seen on New York's subway lines before, prerecorded announcements of the train's next stop, and little lights on a diagram of the stations on that line to tell you where you are and which direction you're going. (They also have noticeably wider doors than the old cars, which ought to speed things up at rush hour.) The voice of the automated announcements does not have a New York accent, sadly, but it does have the virtue of being clear and easy to understand. I'm sure that New Yorkers are already complaining that this clarity takes the fun out of things, and are prematurely pining for the highly personal and unpredictable voices that would squawk, warble, gargle, murmur, shriek, and otherwise pretend to communicate information over a PA system that was always tuned either too soft or way, way too loud.

But automated systems have to work right.

In London a couple of years ago, I was riding one of the new, automated cars on the Northern Line (which used to have the oldest, grottiest cars in the Underground — and still does, sometimes), admiring the improvements to comfort, décor, and clarity of announcements, when I realized that the automated voice was just a few beats off in its timing. The doors would open, people would get on and off, and the doors would be just starting to slide shut when the voice announced the station stop. Still a few bugs in the system.

In Boston, which also recently started using new cars with automated station announcements, I was riding the Red Line in from Braintree and listening to the pre-recorded voice announce, "Next stop: Quincy Adams." Unfortunately, it repeated the same thing at every station—"Next stop: Quincy Adams"—as it left the Quincy Adams stop behind and trundled farther and farther into the heart of the city.

Finding our way through the mess
It's amazing, sometimes, how inadequate the information design can be in a transit system. In Seattle, there is no subway per se, but the transit system spent a huge amount of time and money building an underground bus tunnel through downtown (in which they laid tracks, in case they later decided to run light-rail trains). There are only a handful of stations, but for some reason, each has an entirely different style of signs for the station name. As a friend pointed out when we were talking about the subject of this column, "The first thing I do when I get into a city's transit system is look around and figure out what style of lettering the information is in. Here in Seattle, in the bus tunnel, there *is* no style." Just to make it a little harder, the station names are designed to be easily readable if you're standing in front of them—but not necessarily if you're looking at them at an extreme angle as you come into the station on a bus.

In the San Francisco Bay Area, the original signs in the BART stations are so discreet that they blend into the background (though perhaps they stood out when they were fresh and new). The lettering is actually quite clear, and very well spaced to be readable from any angle; it's just that the signs themselves are too few, too subtly positioned, almost too self-effacing.

More recent, electronic signage in the San Francisco Bay Area's BART *system.*

There is no perfect signage system, just as there is no perfect transit system. We live in unruly, jumbled human agglomerations, which, no matter how huge they may be, are made up of lots of local places and individual people in unique, interlocking communities and neighborhoods. But it's very, very useful when someone can recognize the patterns of all that urban life and translate it into information, and then make that information — simplified, systematized, and clearly marked — available to all the people rushing about their business through the streets and tunnels.

Electoral typography

After the disputed US presidential election of 2000, a look at the effect of bad design in our public life.
[*November 13, 2000*]

THE ELECTION BROUHAHA over the so-called "butterfly ballot" in one county in Florida made it brutally clear that the quality of graphic design has real-world importance.

Design for communication
It seemed obvious when the story broke that it was a matter of bad information design. Good design communicates its message clearly, without ambiguity; the ballot design used in West Palm Beach was certainly an attempt to do that, but it was a failure.

It was one of those hole-punch ballots, the kind where you set the ballot down on a surface that aligns it with a bunch of pegs, and then you use a little pointed metal or plastic tool to punch through the ballot opposite the name of the person you want to vote for. You turn pages until you've gone through all the candidates (or propositions, or whatever) to be voted on, then you remove your ballot and turn it in. Generally, the candidates are listed only on the righthand page.

The designer of this particular ballot was trying to fit a long list of presidential candidates onto a single page (or rather, a single spread) of a fairly short ballot; the way she did it was to put some of the candidates on the lefthand page, and others on the facing righthand page, with the holes to be punched running down the middle. What evidently flummoxed a lot of voters was that to vote for the second candidate on the lefthand page, Al Gore, you had to punch the third hole — because the second hole was meant for the first candidate on the righthand page, Pat Buchanan.

The "butterfly ballot."

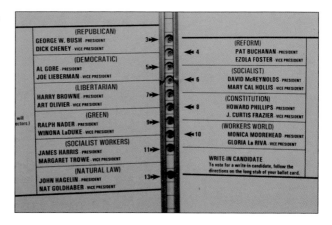

(REPUBLICAN)		
GEORGE W. BUSH · PRESIDENT 3➤		
DICK CHENEY · VICE PRESIDENT	◀ 4	**(REFORM)**
		PAT BUCHANAN · PRESIDENT
(DEMOCRATIC)		EZOLA FOSTER · VICE PRESIDENT
AL GORE · PRESIDENT 5➤		**(SOCIALIST)**
JOE LIEBERMAN · VICE PRESIDENT	◀ 6	DAVID McREYNOLDS · PRESIDENT
(LIBERTARIAN)		MARY CAL HOLLIS · VICE PRESIDENT
HARRY BROWNE · PRESIDENT 7➤		**(CONSTITUTION)**
ART OLIVIER · VICE PRESIDENT	◀ 8	HOWARD PHILLIPS · PRESIDENT
(GREEN)		J. CURTIS FRAZIER · VICE PRESIDENT
RALPH NADER · PRESIDENT 9➤		**(WORKERS WORLD)**
WINONA LaDUKE · VICE PRESIDENT	◀ 10	MONICA MOOREHEAD · PRESIDENT
(SOCIALIST WORKERS)		GLORIA La RIVA · VICE PRESIDENT
JAMES HARRIS · PRESIDENT 11➤		**WRITE-IN CANDIDATE**
MARGARET TROWE · VICE PRESIDENT		To vote for a write-in candidate, follow the
(NATURAL LAW)		directions on the long stub of your ballot card.
JOHN HAGELIN · PRESIDENT 13➤		
NAT GOLDHABER · VICE PRESIDENT		

Is that clear?

I must admit that, when I finally saw a photograph of the ballot in question, I didn't think it was all that hard to figure out how to vote for the candidate you wanted. Arrows pointed from each candidate's name to the appropriate hole; you just had to pay attention to where the arrows were pointing. But as a graphic designer I'm trained to notice the arrangement of graphic elements on a page, and to think about things like the visual hierarchy. This sort of symmetrical arrangement around a central gutter isn't strange to me. To many of the local voters in Florida, it obviously was.

Whether I could figure it out or not, it was not an example of good design. It failed in its purpose; and because of the closeness of the election, that failure has had enormous consequences for the political life of the United States.

Subtly unreadable

I've seen less spectacular examples of bad visual design in politics. I'm not talking about poorly designed posters or bumper stickers; that's too huge a subject to get into now. I'm talking about plain old poor typography.

Many states, counties, or cities publish voters' guides before an election: booklets that list the candidates and propositions and give more or less detail on the people or issues in question. If there are proposed new laws, or changes to existing laws, on the ballot, then the voters' pamphlet may contain quite a lot of text — either the contents of the laws themselves, or commentary on them and statements by supporters and detractors. If the idea is that voters should actually read all this material before making up their minds, then the material should be presented in an inherently readable fashion.

When I perused the San Francisco voters' pamphlet this month (it was the size of a medium-sized city's phone book), I noticed that one of the many propositions to be voted on was harder to read than the rest. The whole book was set in Helvetica, at an ordinary size and with ordinary leading, if somewhat over-long line lengths — nothing terribly inviting, but at least reasonably readable. But in one section, dealing with one of the propositions, all the text was set much tighter; it looked like negative letterspacing had been used, so the letters were all squashed together with almost no space in between. The effect was to make that one proposition and its supporting text much less readable, which in turn made it all the more likely that voters would skip over the fine print of that section.

Since I didn't keep the voters' pamphlet once the election was over, I can't tell you which proposition was so afflicted, or whether it succeeded or failed at the ballot box. But I can tell you that the information in the voters' pamphlet about that particular proposition was made noticeably less accessible than the information about all the other propositions. Enough to make a real difference in the voting? Who knows?

I'm sure it wasn't deliberate — no disgruntled typographer's electoral sabotage. It was probably just sloppiness; someone turned on a tight-tracking command when they

*A recent photo of new signage
in the Düsseldorf airport.*

set that type. I've seen the same kind of mistake before, in a voters' pamphlet in Washington State a few years ago, where the typography of the text was so uninviting that it may have discouraged quite a few voters from familiarizing themselves with all the details on what they were being asked to vote into law.

Design kills

What all this means is that design hurts, when it's done badly. We're not just talking about aesthetics here.

In fact, bad design can kill. Confusing highway signs have undoubtedly led to many a roadside fatality — not to mention a lot of lost time and tempers. One of the most appallingly instructive lessons in the importance of design is the case of the airport at Düsseldorf, in Germany. There was a catastrophic fire in the airport a couple of years ago, in which a number of people died. After the fact, it was determined that some of those people died because the signage in the airport was so bad that they couldn't find their way out. The airport authorities proceeded to hire MetaDesign in Berlin, well-known specialists in information design, to create a system of temporary signage while the airport was being rebuilt — a system that was later expanded into the airport's permanent signage. In September I passed through Düsseldorf airport; I had a hard time finding a cash machine, but by God you could tell where the emergency exits were.

Think it through

The lessons are clear. When you need to communicate something clearly, think clearly about what you want to say. If you're in charge of a public process or a public facility, hire someone who's good at this to design your information system — and make it a real system, consistent and easy to follow.

Not every "designer" is good at this. Too many of us devote too much of our time and effort to developing a style, or to decoration, or to self-expression in the name of creativity. But the effectiveness of good design is easy to gauge: just look at it. Put it to the test. Does it work?

Kerning chads

You wouldn't think that bad kerning could have an effect on electoral politics — but it can.

[February 22, 2002]

IF GOOD TYPOGRAPHY is about communication, and poor typography gets in the way of communication, what happens when the typography in something as real-world as a voters' pamphlet is poorly done?

Trying to read the fine print

Lots of United States cities, counties, and states publish voters' pamphlets when an election is in the offing — thick publications on newsprint that explain who the candidates are and what the propositions and initiatives and other issues will be. It's probably safe to say that most voters don't read these pamphlets very closely, if at all. But in low-profile races, like those for judgeships (in states where judges are elected) or for county assessors or school-board members (at least when the voters aren't parents of school-age children), people who are curious enough or dutiful enough to actually want to find out about the candidates and the issues do look at what's printed in the voters' pamphlets. How much difference does it make whether the text is easy or difficult to read?

In all the voters' pamphlets I've seen, the text is unedited. It's printed exactly as the candidates or backers submitted it — so clarity and good writing have a chance to make a good impression, and the electoral system gives fuzzy thinkers and inarticulate writers enough rope to hang themselves in public. When the issue isn't a candidate but a complicated matter of local law, with statements and counter-statements and misleading double-negatives and perhaps an official explanation of exactly what will change in the wording of the statute in question, there may be an awful lot of fine print to plow through.

A typographer can make the fine print easy to read, or the sort of thing that makes your eyes glaze over and your attention wander. There's a reason why contracts that nobody wants you to read are typeset in 8pt Times Bold in 45-pica lines with almost no leading — and maybe in all-caps, to boot. Electoral documents aren't likely to be as outrageous as that; I've even seen legal requirements that the type has to be at least a certain point size. But nobody sets a requirement about how well that type has to be set.

The devil's in the details

Does this sound like trivia? It is, but the manipulation of that trivia can actually have an effect on an election. It can have an effect whether it's manipulated on purpose (to disguise something and slip it by the voters) or simply through sloppiness and lack of attention to detail. All those fine points of typography that can make text readable and inviting can also make it unreadable and uninviting.

I wish I still had the Washington State voters' pamphlet from a few years ago that first got me thinking about this question. While I'm sure there was no nefarious plot behind it, I noticed that the fine print of some of the initiatives before the voters was set with much tighter tracking than the fine print of some of the others. The effect was to make that text harder to read, because the letters were all squeezed too tightly together.

What I do have is two voters' pamphlets from the California primary election on March 5, 2002: one from the State of California, and one from the City and County of San Francisco.

In the San Francisco pamphlet, most of the text is set in either Helvetica or Times Roman, the default fonts of the western world. The candidates' statements are set in Helvetica in a two-column format that works reasonably well (except for an apparent phobia about hyphens, which leads to some very large gaps between words every now and then), but some of the more general information is set in 10pt or 11pt Helvetica in lines so long that they span the entire width of the letter-size page, and there are boxed notices that have been tracked so tight that nobody could be expected to read them with comprehension.

Detail of Helvetica text from San Francisco voters' pamphlet

Notice to voters registered as Nonpartisan (including Independent, Decline to Stat
ibertarian Party of California has determined that they will not allow Nonpartisan vo
ididates on the Libertarian Party ballot. The Libertarian Party ballot is available only

In the back of the pamphlet, where the texts of proposed changes in the laws are given, they appear in Times Roman at a small size in three justified columns. Although it's clearly "the fine print," it's not that hard to read — except, again, for the lack of hyphenation. "A" for effort, but execution could be better.

Detail of proposed text changes, using Times Roman with underlined and crossed-out passages

officer only pursuant to Section 15.105. Members appointed ~~by the Mayor may be~~

In the California pamphlet, there are no obvious typesetting errors, but there is a very peculiar combination of typefaces. The subheads, which include the candidates' names, are set in a generously spaced sans serif face (Scala Sans, I believe) in semibold caps and small caps; these work remarkably well. But all of the text of the pamphlet is set is Goudy Old Style.

Goudy Old Style & Scala Sans used in the California voters' pamphlet

VALLI SHARPE-GEISLER	I am a moderate and believe in the separation o
Secretary of State	your chief elections official I will: *Help Californ*
	vote by allowing ballot statements for all candida
4718 Meridian Ave., #228	State Senate and Assembly. *Safeguard* against vo

Goudy Old Style is a typeface that we're all used to, so it has the virtue of familiarity. But it's a busy, idiosyncratic face (like most of Frederic Goudy's), and in its photo and digital forms, it's a spindly one too. It became anemic in the transition from letterpress to offset printing. It's got thin, almost vine-like letterforms that appear to grow together if you let them; even when they're not set too closely, I often have the urge to take pruning sheers to the typeface. And this effect is doubled when it comes to the italic.

In the California voters' pamphlet, most of the Goudy Old Style text is set with little or no leading, which makes it hard to read. The tracking in most places is a little tight (though not extraordinarily so), and the line length of the candidates' statements is just a little too long to read comfortably — especially with that lack of leading. But the amazing thing is the texts of proposed laws in the back of the book, which are set entirely in italic. Goudy Old Style has a decorative italic that looks lovely in small doses, but it's a disaster in long blocks of text; I can't imagine anyone but the most persistent and keen-eyed lawyer plowing through these endless patches of dense, spiky undergrowth. (Did I mention the straight quotes and the fake small caps? Maybe I was a bit hasty in saying there were "no obvious typesetting errors.") And of course no one thought to use old-style figures for the recurring blocks of numerals such as seven-digit subsection numbers and large sums of money.

Goudy Old Style Italic used for the text of proposed laws

> *5096.615. The two hundred twenty-five million dollars ($225,000,000) allocated pursuant to subdivision (a) of Section 5096.610 shall be available for appropriation by the Legislature to*

Skip the small stuff?

There's no smoking gun here. It's all small stuff: details. But if we hire skilled designers to pay minute attention to the details of our telephone books (and we do), perhaps we should be doing the same when it comes to the essential tools of our electoral system. It's not just the design of the ballot that counts.

design all around us

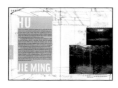

Floating in numbers and letters

The digital becomes physical, and sometimes vice versa, in the exhibition at the San Francisco Museum of Modern Art, "010101: Art in Technological Times."

[*July 13, 2001*]

IN TYPICAL FASHION, I only got around to going to see the SFMOMA exhibition "010101: Art in Technological Times" on the very last weekend before it closed. I wasn't sure what I would find. I knew that the accompanying web site (*010101.sfmoma.org*) had been up and running since before the physical show opened (since the actual date 01/01/01), but what about the in-house exhibits? I had the vague feeling that such a show would all be "digital art" of one sort or another — something high-concept but sort of irritating to view, like certain kinds of intellectual video art. The show was, instead, varied, stimulating, amusing, and well conceived.

Each of the three dozen or so artists took a very different approach to technology and art, but collectively their work did indeed explore the boundary between the physical and the digital. There were a lot of screens set up throughout the exhibit, displaying changing quotations or selections from the "010101" web site, but it was the physical environment that was most striking.

Walking into a room full of square pedestals topped with Karin Sander's miniature humans tends to bring the digital world into physical reality in a disturbingly literal way. Sander had a series of friends and acquaintances stand and be scanned from all sides, then reproduced them at one-tenth scale by extruding thin layers of plastic cross sections and layering them like a human topo map. Add some careful painting of the plastic, to re-create the colors of the actual person and his or her clothes, and you've got in effect little action figures of real people. (Except that, like most real people "sitting" self-consciously for a portrait, the subjects mostly stood in stiff, inert poses and looked vaguely uncomfortable.)

Karin Sander created her miniatures by scanning friends and acquaintances on all sides, then reproducing the images at one-tenth scale.

The effect of Sander's miniatures is heightened when the walls of the room display drawings by Rebeca Bollinger of visual documents found on the Web, rendered as thumbnail-sized pencil drawings, arranged in tiny grids on vellum. The sketches are so tiny that the information contained in the documents is lost, yet until you bend close to look at them they seem to be presenting dense fabrics of information.

Type in technological art

I was fascinated to see how type and letters were used in the various pieces of art, and in the exhibit itself. Many of the art works had no type in them at all, of course.

Where Bollinger's drawings gave the illusion of type, but without content, Tatsuo Miyajima's "Floating Time" used numbers, rather than letters, to create an immersive experience of degrading time: a projection on a floor-screen (which you were encouraged to walk on) of isolated numerals from LED displays, each one in a different size and color, each one appearing at random and then counting down from 9 to 1. A very simple concept, but the effect was to make you feel as though you'd wandered right into cyberspace.

"The Fiction Between 1999 & 2000," by Hu Jie Ming, was a different kind of immersive experience. It consisted entirely of a maze of floor-to-ceiling curtains of transparent photographic film, covered with black-

A portion of Hu Jie Ming's "The Fiction Between 1999 & 2000," as pictured in the exhibit catalog.

and-white screen shots taken from TV screens in the 24 hours of January 1, 2000. Most of these shots, arranged in strict grids that fill the curtains, came from Chinese TV, so most of the printed words you see are in Chinese; interspersed, you find shots from CNN and other Western sources with English words and phrases. Some images are from news reports, others from popular movies or ads or special "millennium" entertainment. Walking among their static images — which you can see from back as well as front — produces another form of confusion between the screen and reality.

John Maeda's "Tap Type Write," which I had seen in action once before during a lecture he gave at the Boston ATypI conference, was one of the interactive prototypes, with a keyboard and screen available to play with. The screen simply shows white dot-matrix letters floating in space, in changing shapes and patterns. Each time you type a letter on the keyboard, the corresponding letter on the screen does something — something well outside the usual behavior of letters. The catalog describes how this mechanism grew out of something that Maeda developed to please his young daughters: "Whenever he was working on the computer, they wanted to play with the keyboard, so he programmed his Macintosh so that something unexpected would happen when they touched the keys: letters would fly, somersault, grow, pulsate, and perform a circus full of acrobatics on the screen."

Text commentary

Surrounding and commenting on these works of art was the signage and the captions that usually punctuate any art exhibit. The accompanying text had its share of pretentious phrases, but it usually did manage to illuminate the art. Reading the caption for meaning and context was often useful — though it was sometimes hard to do, as the text was presented in silver/gray lettering on a black panel. (But as readers of this column may remember [*see*

The exhibit's handy 150-page catalog uses color blocks to set off margins.

"*Room with a view*," page 59], I have a running argument with the way text is displayed in most museum installations.)

The greatest amount of text and type, of course, is to be found in the exhibit's catalog — a remarkably unpretentious little book that costs only ten dollars and can be carried around like a novel. The 150-page catalog measures only 6 inches by a little under 9 inches, and it's printed on uncoated white stock in saturated color. The design draws attention to itself, with its color blocks setting off the margins from the body of the text, but once you get used to it, it works well enough. The one thing that annoys me is that the designer chose an elegant old-style text typeface for the essays and then used spindly-looking, faked small caps to start off each essay. Jonathan Hoefler's Requiem (the typeface in question) is a family with true small caps, extensive ligatures, and even three different versions at different optical sizes; why didn't the designer make use of them? (The catalog entries are in a bold, squarish, highly condensed sans serif that I ought to recognize but don't. No faked small caps there.)

The catalog uses faked small caps to begin each essay, despite the availability of true small caps in the Requiem typeface used.

ACCORDING TO BRIAN ROTMAN IN HIS 1987 BOOK SIGNIFYING NOTHING: THE SEMIOTICS OF ZERO, three parallel developments in Western culture changed our relation to reality beginning in the thirteenth

It's hard to tell what the catalog would mean to someone who hadn't seen the show, but it's a handy little compendium, useful for reference, and of course it does include quite a few essays, along with stage-setting quotations from various sources. The printed photos don't begin to suggest the immersive experience of seeing the art in place, but they draw a connection between the digital and the physical through the tactile medium of the book itself.

Images of most of the art works exhibited in the museum can be found on the "010101" web site, with a little digging in the "about the artists" section. Not all of them are available. Hu Jie Ming's installation has no photographic record, for instance, according to the accompanying copy. Karin Sander's "artist photo," on the other hand, consists of a close-up of her own miniaturized self, as extruded in 1:10 plastic. The "010101" web site remains archived on the SFMOMA site, though it's now buried in the "past exhibitions" area.

The three components of "010101" are the web site, the catalog, and the exhibits themselves set up in the museum. Since the exhibits are no longer in place, we're left with the very appropriate duality of a physical book and an utterly digital web site. Roving back and forth between the two is a rewarding experience.

All art created now is "art in technological times," even art that's rooted in millennia of technique and tradition. "010101" is just a pointer, a way of focusing our attention so we see the interface of ourselves and the digital future.

Room with a view

Why is it that the descriptive captions on the exhibits in art museums are always so hard to read while you're looking at the artwork?

[*January 19, 2001*]

One of those recurring principles of designing with type is to think about where the type will be seen from. How far away is it from the viewer's eye, and at what angle will it be looked at? Will it — or the viewer — be in motion? This problem is doubled when the type is a label next to a work of art displayed in a museum.

Point of view

Every time I walk through an art museum, I get frustrated. No matter how wonderful the art, no matter how well it's displayed, and no matter how brilliant the architecture of the building, there's one thing that always gets short shrift: the descriptive captions next to each piece of art.

The purpose of the caption is to identify the work, and often to give some description of its nature or provenance. With a painting, for instance, there's usually a title, and an artist's name with dates, and perhaps something about where the painting was done and what techniques and materials were used. There may be a sentence or a phrase (or even a short paragraph) about the subject of the painting, or about how it fits into some thematic or chronological sequence that the exhibit is meant to embody. This is all useful information, and most of us welcome it as we browse or concentrate our way through an art exhibit.

But most of the time the captions seem to have been designed to be seen (and read) from one distance, while the art itself needs to be viewed from quite a different distance, a good deal farther away.

Peering at a wall caption that's way too small.

There is an ideal distance for viewing art — though it varies with the individual piece, and with the artistic methods used. In a museum exhibition of Impressionist paintings, for instance, it's very important to stand back far enough for the individual bits of color to mesh and blend into an overall effect. That's what those particular paintings are all about. (You might also want to walk up close and study the details of the brushstrokes and the texture of the paint itself, but for appreciating the painting as a whole, you have to stand back.) It's hard enough, in a crowded museum, to get the distance you need; if the museum's rooms themselves aren't too small, then without exception you'll find that when you stand back from a painting, someone will walk right in front of you and stop in the center of your field of vision.

The ideal viewing distance for a piece of sculpture might be quite different. In an exhibit of, say, fine calligraphy or typography, the ideal viewing distance is probably much closer than for a large painting.

Yet inevitably, no matter what the subject, the captions are made too small, so that you have to keep alternating between a comfortable viewing distance for the art and a (much closer) distance at which you can actually read the information about it.

Integrating art and text

It's a simple question of signage, really, and of information design. But for some reason the same museums that have superb signage to guide you around from one room to another seldom give the same careful attention to the descriptive captions.

There's no one way to design a caption for a museum. But the same principles apply there that apply in any other typographic situation. The typeface needs to be inherently readable; it needs to be spaced correctly; the line lengths shouldn't be too long for absorbing the information at a glance; and the size of the type needs

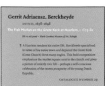

A couple of variations on potential designs for readable museum captions. But it all depends on how big they are, and where they're placed.

to be large enough to be seen from wherever someone is viewing it. There also has to be enough contrast between type and background, and the caption shouldn't be on a shiny surface or behind glass or plastic with a bright light glaring off it.

The biggest problem is size. I suspect that most museum designers think that museum-goers would be put off if the captions were so large that they took up a significant part of the wall real estate. But if the information is important, then it should be seen. If it's not important, then it should be somewhere else, somewhere other than on the wall next to the art—perhaps grouped together as a sort of "fine print" on a plinth or a stele somewhere else in the gallery (not in the line of sight), or buried in the back of a catalog. Making the caption readable while keeping it as unobtrusive as possible is a classic problem of information design.

(It also requires the help of the editors or caption-writers, in deciding what information really is essential and what just gets in the way and clutters up the viewers' experience.)

Type for reading

I'm partial to a good humanist sans-serif type,* for situations like this: something that's got classical bones but is stripped down to essentials, without a lot of contrast between strokes or a lot of distracting flourishes. But not an industrial sans—and certainly not Helvetica, where the similarity of shape among many of the letters (and numbers!) makes it hard to distinguish one from another. (Remember, in a caption for art, you're quite likely to run into unfamiliar names, so you can't rely on familiarity as a tool for recognizing individual letters. They have to be clearly distinguished from each other.)

Syntax would be an obvious choice. Or FF Thesis Sans. Maybe ITC Stone Sans. There are lots of others. (About the worst possible choice would be a version of

*For more about humanist sans-serif typefaces, see the essays in *Dot-font: talking about fonts* (Mark Batty Publisher, 2006).

Bodoni or Didot, unless it was very, very carefully spaced. The fine serifs and the huge contrast between thick and thin strokes make them the antithesis of a typeface for information design.)

I would also use a typeface that has old-style numerals (sometimes called "lowercase" numerals, because their bodies match the x-height and they have ascenders and descenders), so that things like dates don't take on more visual importance than they really deserve. (And so they're more easily readable.)

But more important is spacing. Since the captions may be viewed from an angle, it's essential not to cram the letters too tightly together; but it's also necessary to make sure they hang together as words. The relationship between the line length and the space between lines is crucial. (The longer the line, the more space is needed between one line and the next.) Essentially, the composition of descriptive labels for museum walls is much like typesetting small bits of text. We're looking at the museum captions from a much greater distance than we would look at the captions on a printed page, but the visual relations are the same. The type size should be large enough to give the same effect, at ten or fifteen feet away, as smaller type on a page would give at a distance of fifteen or twenty inches.

Brownian motion

Take a look at the captions, next time you walk through an art museum. Take along your trifocals, or you computer reading glasses, if you're middle-aged like me. And be prepared to do the art museum two-step, shuffling back to see the art, and forward to read the caption. I suppose it's good exercise.

One for all?

An ambitious mass-market magazine launched at the end of the dot-com boom, ONE claimed as its motto, "Design Matters." Although the magazine didn't last, the idea behind it was a good one.

[*January 12, 2001*]

THE YEAR 2000 WAS A FERTILE MOMENT for new design magazines, but the most ambitious may have been ONE, the high-concept magazine-*cum*-web-site launched in December in San Francisco. ONE (complete with all-uppercase name) was the brainchild of Dana Lyon, a former publisher of *Wired*, and it was aimed squarely at the same demographic.

All about design
Before the first issue even hit the stands, ONE had achieved a certain amount of unsettled buzz in the publishing world for going through three editorial directors. This may have reflected the ambiguities and contradictions of the magazine's goal: to be a design-centered magazine that reaches out far beyond the specialist world of designers and design writers, to the much wider audience of people who consume design.

The conception of ONE was based on the quite accurate observation that design is everywhere, and the concommitant desire to celebrate it. The 20th century may well have been characterized by our first real awareness that we live largely in a designed environment. But if our present society doesn't self-destruct, from the 21st century on we'll be much more conscious of the fact that we're creating and altering and morphing and modifying ourselves and all the world we live in — so we might as well pay some attention to designing it. (That's what design is: planning, thinking ahead, thinking things through.) Making people more aware of design, and helping them think about it, is an admirable idea — and it might even be a way to make a lot of money.

But how do you go about talking to people about design?

Tangled in the girders

I had an intensely ambivalent reaction to ONE. Much as I like the idea of integrating a printed magazine with an online publication, I was not too impressed with the cluttered web site as I first saw it. Too much style, not enough substance. And the style wasn't very...well, stylish. The graphic cornerstone of ONE, as reflected in its logo, seemed to be an Erector Set construction of lots of rectilinear bars and squarish rectangles; and this was the dominant look of the web site. Rather than focusing our attention or working with various types of contrast, this presented the whole thing as a jumble.

The web site later evolved into something that seemed a little more solid (though it was still awfully busy, and it committed the unpardonable sin of having animated ads that wouldn't scroll off the screen). The printed magazine had a little of the same problem with focus, but it also afforded a wider canvas, and some of its individual layouts looked lively and strong. (I certainly don't mean to suggest that the only designs that work are big, simple ones without a lot of detail. But, to paraphrase ONE's subtitle: "structure matters.") Like most first issues, this one attempted a lot of things, and some of them failed.

Types of design

Typographically, ONE is squarely of its time. The typefaces, according to the colophon at the back of the magazine, are all from FontShop: FF Eureka and Eureka Sans,
and FF Minimum. (I'm always pleased to see a proper
colophon at the back of a magazine, giving the details of
printing, paper, and typography, but this one has an odd
way of expressing itself: "Typography from FontShop
International," it says, before listing the fonts and their
designers. But of course what FontShop supplied was
the typefaces; the "typography" was in the way they were
used.)

FF Minimum has been around for a while (it was
designed 1993–95 by Pierre di Sciullo), but I haven't seen
it used that widely. It's one of those typefaces that takes
boxiness and pixel-based angularity to extremes. ONE
uses it for small headlines and running typographic elements — but for the most part only the basic, straightforward "Noir" version of Minimum, which is easy enough
to read. (The type family actually includes a bewildering,
almost fractal set of variants.) ONE's logo, created by
Abbott Miller, is clearly in the same spirit — although in
the logo, the horizontal strokes are narrower than the
vertical strokes, to give a certain lightness and horizontal
movement, whereas in the typeface Minimum they're
strictly equal. (The logo's structure of overlapping translucent girders was modified on the cover of the first issue
into three plain white letters — a much stronger graphic
image against a busy background.) The use of Minimum
in small ways weaves the square sensibility throughout
the magazine.

FF Eureka is a more recent release, especially in its
sans-serif version. (It was also used at around the same
time in the first issue of a much smaller, less commercial
magazine about typography and design: *dot-dot-dot*.)
Eureka was designed as a large serif/sans type family by
the Slovakian type designer Peter Bil'ak — and, although

ONE didn't have much need of this feature, it's available in a Central European version with all the accents and other diacritical marks needed for Polish, Hungarian, Czech, Slovak, and so on.

Eureka is a mix of the sturdy and the clunky. It has a bit of the angular sturdiness of many Dutch oldstyle typefaces, with some of the clunky shapes and gawky forms of late-19th-century attempts at oldstyles. There's not much contrast between the strokes. It's a little like a combination of the original Cheltenham and FF Scala, with a narrower body than either. The serif version reminds me quite a bit of Kurt Weidemann's Bible-typeface, ITC Weidemann, except that Eureka isn't quite as condensed and has a much smaller x-height. With its sort of wedge/ slab serifs and abrupt angles, Eureka has much more style at large sizes than in text, but as a text face it's quite readable. I confess that its style in text simply doesn't appeal to me, but it's obviously deliberate.

FF Eureka Sans, which is shorn of the attention-grabbing serifs, looks much more contemporary. It's used in ONE extensively for captions and small text, where it has the clarity and even texture you'd expect. (Interestingly, in both the serif and sans versions of Eureka, the bold weight is much wider and more rounded than the semi-condensed roman. And the italics of both are notably narrow and compact.)

Falling into the perfect gutter

The first issue of ONE was a thick magazine, chock full of ads. At 192 pages, on stock that's noticeably less flimsy than some current magazines (60# Mead Vision Velvet, to be precise — thanks again to the colophon), ONE obviously needed a spine. It would be nearly impossible to saddle-stitch that many pages — and the trend these days is to perfect-bind any magazine you possibly can, whether it needs a spine or not. ("Perfect-binding" is a misleading term for the same binding method that's used

Some of the text gets lost in the gutter

Translucent overlay between pages with Frank Gehry sketches

in cheap paperback books: trim off the inner folds of the signatures and glue the inner edges to a flat backing.) But like so many current magazines, ONE didn't really take into account the effect of perfect-binding on the page design.

In a perfect-bound magazine, unlike one that's been saddle-stitched (stapled on the fold at the spine), the pages can never open completely flat. The inner edges always curve into shadow where they're glued to the spine. It's all very well to design a beautiful two-page spread that looks breathtaking on your double-wide monitor and in mock-ups and color proofs, but the reality is that whatever you let run into the gutter is going to disappear. If you're going to run display type or an image across the gutter, you have to take into account what the pages will really look like when your readers are holding it in their hands or on their laps. (Maybe you can somehow make the fact of losing part of the image in the middle become integral to the design. Or you could overlap them slightly — but this is tricky. At the very least, make sure that nothing crucial is in the lost area.)

In one instance, the designers of ONE made good use of this awkward binding method, by inserting a single sheet of translucent yellow paper in the middle of the opening spread of an article on Frank Gehry; on the yellow sheet is reproduced a scrawled sketch of Gehry's, which begins on the lefthand page and complements the photograph on the righthand page. But in many other instances, all the stuff running into the gutter is just distracting and frustrating.

Maybe it's time for a campaign to return to the spineless magazines of yesteryear. And I do wish someone would start writing regularly, and critically, about the design of current magazines; it's a fertile ground. (What a great way to lose friends and influence people!)

The design lifestyle

ONE seemed to embrace pretty much everything. It had the feel of a lifestyle magazine (significantly, its promo to distributors said, "Display next to: *Vanity Fair*, *Wired*, *Wallpaper*"), where everyone is stylish and even the humans have the look of consumables. It's worth noting how many of the objects exposed in ONE's pages had price tags attached. There was an awful lot of *product* in there. When the photos of people are annotated with detailed lists of the clothing they wear and who made it and where you can buy it, you know you're in the realm of fashion.

That's the problem. It was hard to find any distinction, in ONE, between design and fashion. "Every designed object has a story to tell," said the magazine's intro, and that's a fine way to approach design for a wide consumer market. But the best way to spread knowledge of a subject is to have a firm, clear core of understanding about the heart of the subject, and then let the edges leak outward in every possible way. You don't need to be rigorously theoretical or to write dry insider jargon to be serious, but you do need to have a definite critical perspective. And open borders.

Is fashion the same as design? No. The two are intertwined, often enough, but they are utterly different things. I think it's important to make the distinction, and I didn't see ONE doing enough of that.

From the start, the danger was that ONE would turn into just an undifferentiated "lifestyle" view of design — and unfortunately, that's pretty much what it did. If a magazine like this can use people's taste for fashion and style as a hook to introduce them to the design behind all those surfaces, then it's doing something worthwhile. If it turns into a glorified catalog...well, the racks are full of them.

PARA

PHRASES ERASMI RO-
terodami in omnes epistolas Pauli apostoli
germanas, & in eam quæ est ad Hebræos
incerti autoris, cum ijs quæ canonicæ uocan
tur rursus ab eo recognitæ absolutæq; po-
stremo à nobis accuratius excusæ, di-
gestæq; per tomos, ut cuiq; ser
care in formam enchiri
dij, si uelit, libe-
rum sit.
BASILEÆ APVD IOANNEM
FROBENIVM,
AN. M. D. XXI.

design on the page

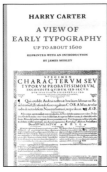

Cover (top) of the Hyphen Press edition; title page (above) of the original edition

Where type came from

One of the clearest, most informative books about early typography is back in print.
[*October 17, 2003*]

NOT MANY BOOKS with scholarly footnotes, and a title that begins *A View of…*, would be considered must-have resources for the modern graphic designer or type user. After all, how much of the minutiae of cutting metal punches in Renaissance France or Reformation Germany will come in useful when you're faced with a deadline for that product catalog or annual report? But Harry Carter's book, *A View of Early Typography: Up to About 1600*, republished in 2003 by Hyphen Press, is the exception. If you care anything about the history — the context — of the craft we all practice, then you'll be richly rewarded by reading this book.

Carter deals quietly and calmly with his subject, in a written voice that must recall his spoken voice (the five main chapters were originally given as lectures at Oxford in 1968) and that is direct, clear, and utterly un-fussy. I have no idea what Harry Carter was like in person (he died in 1982), but I can imagine sitting comfortably in a room with him and — apart from the necessary apparatus of a slide presentation (the talks were illustrated, as the book is) — simply listening to him talk.

His subject is the first hundred and fifty or so years of making and using movable type. More specifically, he is interested in how you can tell what types were used in early books, who cut them and cast them, and what that can tell us about who they were and where they came from. Carter is looking at a very specific set of crafts, but he puts the story in the context of its time and place: western and central Europe at a moment of intense cultural revival, political striving, and violent religious confrontation. Being a printer or a punchcutter or a type founder in those days was not necessarily a safe job.

"The face comes loose from the metal"
Carter's opening chapter, "The Technicalities of Type," starts off with the famous first line, "Type is something that you can pick up and hold in your hand." At the time he wrote, before digital type and when phototypesetting was just becoming popular, this was already a point that he felt it was important to make. Speaking of those who study old books, he went on: "Bibliographers mostly belong to a class of people for whom it is an abstraction: an unseen thing that leaves its mark on paper. For their convenience it has long been the practice to talk about a typeface, meaning, not the top surface of a piece of type, nor even of many pieces of assembled type, but the mark made by that surface inked and pressed into paper." In the following pages, Carter explains how type was actually made, not just mechanically but historically, and how the various tasks involved got divided up, and later brought together again.

One of his points is that type foundries, which we think of as "where type gets made" and which we have morphed into today's digital foundries, started out as a bunch of separate jobs being done by different people in several businesses. I have never read a better explanation of what it meant to cut punches, to use them to make matrices (impressions of what's carved on the end of the punch), and to put each matrix into an adjustable mould and use that to cast type. It wasn't until the middle of the 16th century, according to Carter, that these tasks started to be done under the same roof. There was a lively trade in punches, and in matrices, as well as in finished type, across much of Europe. In this process there was also a great deal of room for variation, intentional or otherwise, which is how a popular type design might spread

Early French types, including a New Testament in French rather than the usual Latin

across several countries, but the "same" typeface might look different when used by each city's printer.

Fewer forms, more readers

Carter's next two chapters, "Diversity of Letter-forms in Print" and "The Establishment of Common Idioms," explain the enormous variety in the styles of handwriting then current — often different styles written by the same person for different purposes — and how this first got translated into a bewildering variety of type styles, then later got narrowed down into a few standard styles (partly as a result of the centralization of type-founding) used for standard purposes. It wasn't just a matter of "blackletter in Germany, roman and italic in Italy"; in an age when much of the printed matter had a propaganda purpose, or at least a few political implications, the style of type in which it was presented made a difference.

The fourth chapter, "Latin and Vernacular," gets into the way printing and type were used to disseminate culture, and the implications of whether it was done in Latin or in the local tongue — and the expectations that readers had about which typeface would be used for each. In 1527, king François I of France ordered that a French translation of Thucydides' *History* be printed, as part of a programme for "enriching, magnifying, and publishing the French language." The translator, who was also a diplomat and a churchman, "recommends the literary use of French as an aid to national aggrandisement and the consolidation of the king's possessions." As Carter points out, this is precisely what was done.

Cutting letters

Carter concludes with "The History of Typefounding and Punchcutting," which goes into a lot of detail but uses it to show how ideas, tools, and small pieces of metal moved around Europe, and he adds a "Supplement on Italic," which was not one of the original lecture series.

Steel punches and a variety of typefaces in use

Italic began as a separate style of type, used to set entire books, based on common forms of literary handwriting in Italy; only in the late 16th century did italic start to be subservient to roman, used as a complementary but secondary typeface, until, as Carter says, "After 1600 no punchcutter offered a Roman face without a companion Italic." And there, at the end of the 16th century, he stops.

A View of Early Typography is generously illustrated, with 84 numbered plates at the back of the book; the captions carefully note whether the examples of printed types shown are at their original size or have been reduced. There's a page of clearly drawn diagrams showing the parts of a piece of type, as well as photographs of moulds and punches and matrices; there is also a chart of the old named type sizes (long before they were standardized, much less given numbers in points), and at the end a very useful map of the printing centers of Europe in 1476.

Harry Carter's book has been out of print for years, so it's a delight to have this new, well-made edition, done as a facsimile of the original printing, with a new introduction by the equally erudite and clear-writing James Mosley and a few additional notes that either correct errors in Carter's text or add more recent information. (Oddly, they missed one mistake in the original: the reference on page 124 to "Fig. 83" should clearly be to Figure 84, the final figure in the book.) Like most Hyphen Press books, this one is printed and bound in a way that makes it comfortable to hold and to read, and that ought to make it last a long time.

F. T. MARINETTI FUTURISTA

ZANG
TUMB TUMB

ADRIANOPOLI   OTTOBRE 1912

*Designed by Italian Futurist
Filippo Tommaso Marinetti
in 1914*

Avant-garde page design

How artists and designers questioned the nature of the
printed page in the first half of the 20th century, and
what this means for designers today.

[*July 8, 2002*]

WHAT IS A PAGE? In particular, what is a page as a design
unit, a frame for art and information, a medium of communication? This is a question that cutting-edge writers
and artists were beginning to ask at the end of the 19th
century (beginning, perhaps, with Stéphane Mallarmé's
arrangements of his poems on the printed page) and
that is being asked again as we move into a digital world
where much of our communication is done on the flick-
ering surface of a computer screen.

    In the course of the 20th century, the printed page
has been expanded, shrunk, turned around, uprooted,
deconstructed, and rebuilt along radically different lines,
by dozens of book artists and graphic-design pioneers,
working in a plethora of schools and movements and
individual situations. Jaroslav Andel's *Avant-Garde Page
Design 1900–1950* (New York: Delano Greenidge Editions,
2002) gives an overview of this process during the first
half of the century, when tradition was being questioned
and Modernism was in flower. Many of the images
reproduced in this large book will look familiar, from
other books and articles on modern design, but here
they're brought together in a compendium laced with
a coherent text (in three languages). The well-printed
illustrations can provide new inspiration for graphic
designers, as well as making us aware of just how much
experimental work has already been done.

Artists and movements on the page
The chapter titles give some indication of how the book
is organized. Beginning with "Precursors and Pioneers"

Designed by Russian Constructivists Georgi and Vladimir Stenberg in 1930

(such as Mallarmé), it proceeds thematically rather than chronologically, with chapters on topics such as "Architecture on the Page," "The Photomechanical Page," and "The Cinematic Page." Themes overlap — architecturally inspired pages often include photographs, for instance — but the groupings make sense, and they give us a structure for dealing with such a mass of graphic material.

Some chapters focus on specific movements, such as Dada or the Futurists, because they came early (before and during the First World War) and because they had such a huge effect on others. The very last chapter deals with the page as pure art, in "artist's books," with the work of Henri Matisse and Marcel Duchamp.

There's a vast variety here. The intentionally disruptive, chaotic pages of scrambled words by the Futurist founder Marinetti contrast with the starkly practical New Typography of Jan Tschichold. Some of the most beautiful and dramatic pages are the work of the Russian Constructivists, with their industrial exhortations in black, white, and red. It helps to be able to read Cyrillic type to appreciate them fully. Indeed, only a reading ability in several languages would make this book completely appreciable, since the examples are taken from a variety of European countries and the words on the pages may be in English, Czech, German, Spanish, Russian, French, or Italian. The captions translate any titles there may be, which is helpful, but they don't attempt to translate the full text of what's shown in each illustration. (For example, on page 201 one of the illustrations is captioned "Title page of 'Flugblätter mit dem Buntquadrat' [Leaflets with the Motley Square], no. 1, 1924," but you have to read German to understand that the text is about what makes good design in advertising. A provocative opening sentence like "Advertising is the handwriting of entrepreneurs!" makes me wish my German were better.)

*Designed by John Heartfield
in 1931*

New media, then and now

The use of photography in print, on the same page as lettering or type, was new and exciting in the early 20th century. It's not unusual today, but it's still very effective, because of the contrast between the texture of type and the visual nature of photographs. This kind of contrast is even carried over into video animation, where the collage of moving words and pictures still relies at least partly on the fundamental contrast between the two forms of visual communication.

Andel's introduction ties these developments together in the context of our current moment, here in the early 21st century:

"The introduction of the printed page and the painted picture to the computer screen is the latest in a series of countless artistic and technological developments that advanced the ways in which pictures and texts are interconnected, produced, transmitted, and received. Originating in crossovers between the fields of art, science, and technology, these inventions were often deeply intertwined. Going back to the nineteenth century, and continuing through the twentieth, photography, the telegraph, the telephone, motion pictures, television, the fax, the computer, and the internet have depended on contributions made by artists, architects, film directors, and designers."

Pages on pages

Since the subject of this book is the printed page, it's interesting to see how the book designer (Enzo Cornacchione) deals with the pages of this book itself. The trilingual text runs in three blocks across the pages, in the same sans-serif typeface but in three different weights — English on top (light), French in the middle (medium), German on the bottom (bold). But not all the text pages carry all three languages. Sometimes only one, or two, of the languages is displayed on a particular page, with the other third or two-thirds of the space taken up by illustrations. The effect is to intersperse the text throughout the highly illustrated chapters, beginning at the same point and ending at the same point but not necessarily taking the same path to get there. This technique also disguises the inevitable problem that the same text will run longer or shorter in some languages than in others. (Since English tends to be the shortest, the typographer could have improved the readability of the English text, and at the same time made it slightly longer, by loosening up the rather tight letter spacing of the lightest weight of type.)

One final quibble: the index only lists the names of people, not of organizations or schools or publications. If you want to find references to the German radical magazine *A.I.Z.*, for instance, you have to know that it was designed by John Heartfield, and go look up his name in the index. An index of proper names is never enough.

Two different kinds of double-page book spreads

Having designs on books

[Part 1 of 3] A designer's perspective on how the books we read end up looking the way they do.
[*April 27, 2001*]

BOOKS ARE STILL the most common way of communicating large amounts of information to a large number of people. Book design, like typography, is one of those things we take for granted unless we practice them professionally; most of us, as readers, don't consciously notice how a page is laid out unless it reaches out and grabs us by the eyeballs. But our ability to enjoy and use books is dependent on the art and the craft of the book designer.

This is the first of three essays about book design. First, let's set the stage; later, we'll look at the fine print.

A book is an object
The basic unit of book design is the page spread. As Swiss book designer Jost Hochuli among others has pointed out, no matter how asymmetrical the layout of the pages may be, they always come in pairs: left and right of the same size and the same aspect ratio, centered on the gutter where they are bound together at the spine. So it makes sense to design with the two-page spread in mind, not just the single page. (This may change someday if we end up with books that coalesce page by page on a single sheet of "smart paper," since there would no longer be any reason except habit to create facing pages; but this is a concern for the future, and maybe for electronic books today.)

This page spread doesn't exist in isolation, either. It's part of an actual physical object in your hands. Book design includes the materials the book is made of — paper, ink, binding, covers, maybe dustjacket — and the size, shape, flexibility, and heft of the book itself. Too often, the designer has no control over any of these physical concerns, because the publisher has already decided on a format and on the materials to be used, but they're nonetheless important. The volume should open easily and the pages should lie reasonably flat while you're reading — something that's hard to achieve with today's binding methods, even in the "sewn" bindings.

The interior of a book (as opposed to its cover, which may be displayed in many ways on a shelf) is going to be viewed from a fairly consistent distance: the convenient distance for holding the book before your face or in your lap, or for laying it down on a table or propping it up on a desk or other nearby surface. The usual distance is about fourteen to eighteen inches; certainly you wouldn't normally try to read a book from a distance of less than a foot or more than two feet, unless you're exceptionally nearsighted or farsighted. (You might peer closely at some detail of a photo or a painting reproduced in a book, or if you're a typographer like me you might study some fine point of the text type, but that's a special case.)

Three ways of looking at a book
Before you can design a book, you need to know its purpose. How will it be used? After all, the designer's client may be the publisher, but the ultimate user of a book is the reader. It's hard — probably impossible — to design a book successfully if you don't read books yourself. As with any other kind of design, you have to be able to put yourself in the mind of the user.

Most books are used in one of three ways: browsing, continuous reading, or reference. (Of course, a single book may be used in all three ways, by different readers or at different times. We've probably all found ourselves browsing through a dictionary just for fun, and I've even been known to read continuously in a book about computer software if it's written entertainingly. The latter, however, probably marks me off as an anomaly

*Browsing: a page spread
from a highly visual book
with sections of big text*

*Continuous reading: a page
spread from a book of essays*

and therefore not to be trusted.) Treatment of type, use
of color, and layout of the page may be quite different for
each kind of book.

Browsing. A book designed for browsing can be much
looser and more flamboyant in its typography and design
than a book meant to be read from end to end. Varying
sizes and styles of type may be appropriate, and there
may be quite a few different kinds of visual and textual
elements mixed up on the pages. (The most obvious are
photographs and drawings, but they may include charts,
graphs, tables, and lists, as well as completely gratuitous
shapes or colors.) You may choose graphic elements
just for their ability to catch the reader's attention, but
you have to give that reader a reward for being caught.
There's a certain necessary hierarchy even in a book
meant purely for browsing; elements that function in
the same way ought to look recognizably related to each
other, and the larger, more eye-catching elements should
lead to finer, more detailed information in some clear
way. Browsing doesn't mean a complete lack of structure.

Continuous reading. Books for continuous reading,
such as novels, histories, or biographies, make up the
hard core of book typography. This is the test: creating
plain blocks of text, page after page of them, that look
inviting and that a reader can plow through happily without strain and without giving a thought to how the page
is designed or what the typeface looks like. Sometimes
books for continuous reading have headings and subheads and other elements that stand out from the flow,
but the heart of the matter is the text itself.

Reference. In a reference book, the reader's paramount
need is to be able to find the information, quickly and
without running up blind alleys. The writer or editor
is responsible for the actual quality of the information and its logical organization, but it's up to the book
designer to make that organization clear and obvious to
the reader. As researchers, we may be willing to put up

*Reference: a page spread from
a software reference manual*

with ugly or cramped text in a reference book, as long as we can get to the right entry easily; after all, we're not expecting to spend a lot of time poring over the prose. But woe to the book designer who chooses a hard-to-read typeface for the key words of a dictionary or encyclopedia!

Two examples

A couple of books worth mentioning at this point show completely different approaches to page design — and they're both on relevant subjects, too.

Revival of the Fittest: Digital Versions of Classic Typefaces, edited by Philip B. Meggs and Roy McKelvey (New York: RC Publications, 2000), comprises a series of essays on various groupings and categories of historical typefaces that have been revived in digital form. So ostensibly this might be a book for continuous reading. But the design is anything but conservative and text-based. Every page is full of colorful illustrations and dramatically shaped blocks of text, along with captions, blown up and interwoven paragraphs, and large and small examples of type in action. Each double-page spread is designed separately, although with a consistent style. This book is highly visual, and it's meant to be browsed.

Since I was involved in the book's creation, as a sort of technical editor of the text, I won't try to write any sort of criticism or analysis. Some might argue that the visual flamboyance is gratuitous, and there are certainly some treatments of the text that I wouldn't do myself. But there's no question that the look is eye-catching, or that there's a lot of information packed into those pages.

Richard Hendel's *On Book Design* (New Haven & London: Yale University Press, 1998) is also visual where it has to be, since its subject is the design of books. Yet Hendel's book (he designed it himself) is comfortable to hold — tall, but lightweight and somewhat narrow — and easy to read straight through. The central text columns are spacious and unvarying, with smaller columns on the outsides of the pages for notes and a lot of little epigraphs quoted from various other sources (sometimes amplifying Hendel's points, sometimes contradicting them); illustrations either fit in the text column or take up the whole width of the page, sometimes on a page by themselves. Since the latter half of the book consists of essays by (or interviews with) eight other book designers, usually focusing on how they did an individual book, there's an obvious usefulness to enclosing such varied approaches within a consistent, continuous *mise-en-page*.

WYNTON M[...]
acclaimed jaz[...]
as well as the[...]
(JALC). Mr. N[...]
awarded the [...]
his work *Bloo*[...]
   Born near[...]
18, 1961, Mr.[...]

Book design: text

[Part 2 of 3] The heart of book design — unflashy but essential — is text spacing and typeface selection.
[*May 4, 2001*]

LET'S TAKE A LOOK at the core of every book: its text.

Text type
The most important thing about text type to keep in mind is that everything affects everything else. Whatever typeface you choose, it's the relationship of type size, letterspacing, word spacing, leading, line length, and margins that makes all the difference between something you can read comfortably and something you'll put down and never come back to.

It's easy to see how the size of the type relates to the leading (the space between the lines, usually measured from baseline to baseline). The more space there is between the lines of type, the easier it is to distinguish one line from the next, and the less likely your eye is to get confused and slip from one line to another at the wrong time. (If the typeface has a large x-height — the height of a lowercase letter that has no ascending or descending stroke — it will appear larger than a typeface with a small x-height at the same point-size. But even typefaces with small x-heights need some extra space between the lines, so their ascenders and descenders don't run into each other.)

It's harder to see how letterspacing (the space between the letters) and word spacing (the space between the words) relates to this. In any given typeface, there's a very narrow range of possible spacing between letters that looks right and feels comfortable to read. Ideally, the type designer has chosen the optimum spacing in designing the font, but sometimes a little variation can help. (I'm usually a purist on this particular topic. There is a proper

Design of a page spread from a book of essays

amount of space between the letters of each typeface, and it shouldn't be allowed to vary. But digital fonts don't always respect the original spacing that the designer had in mind, at least when the digital font is an adaptation of a typeface that was first designed in metal.) Since the space within a letter and the space around it ought to be in harmony, a thin, light typeface should actually be spaced more loosely than a thick, bold face. (Because the open spaces inside a bold letter are actually smaller than the open spaces within a light version of the same letter.) This seems counterintuitive, but it's true.

Since the space around the word is related to the space within the word, it makes sense that a line of type floating in a huge blank space could be letterspaced a little more loosely than the same line of type tucked snugly into a paragraph of prose. For the same reason, the space between words might be slightly — slightly! — wider in the line floating in space, to match the looser letterspacing. But the space between words should always be fairly tight: just enough to clearly separate one word from the next, without creating big gaps that the reader's eye can fall into. (The most common problem is narrow columns of justified text, such as we all see every day in newspapers: these almost guarantee poor word spacing, and sometimes poor letterspacing too, which makes the text much harder to read.)

The longer the line of text, the more space is needed between lines. You can get away with setting text in long, long lines of small type if you give them enough space between the lines — lots of space between the lines. But for ordinary reading, in paragraphs, there are various studies of the optimum number of words or letters on a line of text; the rule of thumb is about 60 letters, or ten "average" words of five characters plus a space. (The real number depends on the actual text, including the writer's choice of words and what kind of prose it is.)

The margins are simply the amount of visual space around the block of text. Obviously, this has an effect on the reader's perception of the text itself, but only really extreme differences will change the way we perceive the spacing within the text block. For the most part, margins are a matter of page layout more than of text typography.

It's important to keep in mind, though, that the real margins aren't necessarily the ones that show up nice and neatly on our computer screens. Since books are real, physical objects, bound down the middle with glue or thread, a small part of the inner margin is always going to be lost, because it's buried in the slope of the pages toward the spine. It's an unfortunately common error in books (and magazines) to forget this visual constriction; the result is pages that seem to run into the gutter, and that are hard to read.

A "real" spread, as it appears in an open book, with curved spine & gutter

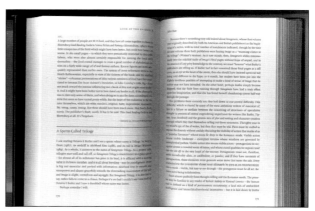

Text typefaces

You might think that I've left out the most important part of designing the text in a book: the typeface. But there are lots of books and articles and bits of advice on which typefaces work best in continuous prose, and why; what I want to impart is some principles of how to use those typefaces, whatever they are, on the pages of a book.

That said, I can suggest a few pointers. Look for type-faces that were designed for text setting, not for display or for advertising. (ITC Garamond, for instance, is a fine type family for setting ads and brochures — which is what it was designed for — but it has very little to do with the various book faces that bear the name Garamond.) Don't be seduced by the notion that a bigger x-height makes a typeface more readable; our eyes see the visual space between lines as the space between the bodies of the lowercase letters, no matter how long or short the ascenders or descenders may be, so a face with a large x-height just has to have more generous leading. Look for a typeface whose letter shapes are based on traditional forms, for the simple reason that we're used to reading them. A text face should also have clearly differentiated letter forms; if the letters are based too closely on the same shapes (like many geometrical faces), then it will be hard to distinguish them in running text.

For typesetting books, it's useful to choose a type family with a truly comprehensive set of members. A book face should always include old-style figures and true small caps, as well as a full set of ligatures. If your design is going to require italic small caps, make sure the typeface includes them. (Most don't.) If you're designing a cookbook, or an art catalog that gives the dimensions of paintings in inches, be sure your typeface has real fractions, and real superior and inferior numerals so you can construct any fractions that aren't already in the font. (There's nothing more irritating than faked fractions, where the numbers have simply been shrunk down so they look light and spindly — and then haven't been spaced properly either. Well, all right, there is something more irritating: decimals where fractions belong. Have you ever actually heard someone say "eight point five by eleven inches"?)

Book design: display

[Part 3 of 3] Taking on display type, front and back matter, and playing nice with others.
[May 11, 2001]

BOOKS MAY BE centered on their text, but what about more prominent words that get a big treatment? What about display type?

Display type

At a glance, it's easy to say what "display type" is: anything that's not running text. But there are lots of different ways to use display type in a book, from the subtle to the splashy. As with any other aspect of book design, the display type should not be just a place for the designer to show off; it should serve a purpose for the reader.

The most straightforward kind of display type is heads, which are attached to the text and serve to guide the reader around. Technical books, in particular, love to revel in a downpour of head styles and sizes and variations, which are intended to reflect the complex organization of the information the book presents. But how many levels of head and subhead does any reader truly pay attention to and distinguish? From my own experience, I'd say the maximum is three — and that limiting the heads to two levels, one big and one small, is better still, while sticking to just a single level of head is best.

Most readers simply want to know what part of the book goes with what other part, and they use heads as a tool for navigating through the text to find the part they're interested in. Subtle distinctions between fourth- and fifth-level heads are simply lost on most people, no matter how carefully the editor may have worked them out, or how brilliantly the designer may have set them off from each other. After all, we don't talk in heads and

Major head

Igna aliquamin delit hommy nisim adiam vent urpatue velestrud minibh nuiscil doles sim ennt praestrud esgiamc onumisnel or perit praestrud tis diputatomy tim nonulla facil ipsusum quicabus euis nullut ipsuscin vel ut ad nat, commodio conved euis venit for alissim dipis adio duisit ad magnim equat, qui sum zzriure minisl inibh exit, sis amet vel eu consdlignat ulluipat nibh eu augat velesum nulla adiesse facilis aliquisl utetum venim incipit la feu facip ex eugait, cor secte dolobor tionsecte volobor uendignia faccum dolore doloripse ncipit nulputpat nis nulla aut dolobrorem dis dolor si ero odolore doloborer feu facilllandre eugait lut lupiat. Ro os nos vullam, quam velit, vel iliquis at, conse vel- iquis dolupptate molobouent, si te tatis exe- quamet, volor uisl exeril exersu eum ivit vulla sim eugait delis zzulliunsan eugait, sustrud modio dunt dunt atem ver si.

Subhead

Metuae in henit pratio erit, consectet prae- sent aliscidui min nos versim in henibh exer at. Eros acin endit exis dsit acipisum san- diam, vullum sfin duis eugait lupitat volor euscilismom hendip et augait et alit adigna consed dismsent eugue sinisl dlanduresti se- tie, sectem quat, consectem diatm, vulpu- tatoe facio urpat adamist nonse re etum

One way of treating different levels of heads on a text page

subheads, and how many of us pore through complicated outlines for fun?

When I'm talking about heads, I mean heads within the text — not chapter titles or subtitles, which are conceptually separate. (I know that some publishers like to number their heads starting with the chapter title, as level one, but this has never made any intuitive sense to me, and I would discourage it.)

To distinguish different levels of head, it's best to use two kinds of contrast at the same time: not just a change of type size, for instance, but a change of type size and a different position on the page, or a change of size and a change of weight or style.

Don't rely too heavily on differences in type style, such as changing from roman to italic, or from a serif to a sans-serif typeface. It's amazing how much a reader doesn't notice unless it's made obvious. A favorite device is to use Helvetica for a run-in sidehead (that is, a subhead that's run into the text, rather than sitting above it or beside it) in a paragraph of Times Roman text. Despite the obvious differences in the letter structure of the two typefaces when you look at them closely, they don't stand out from each other enough in a page of text; the change just creates an impression of clutter and disorder. If you add a change of weight to the change of style, however, then you've created enough contrast to make the difference obvious: Helvetica Bold (better yet, Extrabold) subheads in regular-weight Times Roman text would stand out quite clearly.

Text is more important than display

Since the text block — the rectangle formed by the lines of text on the page — is presumably designed for easy reading, the display type shouldn't intrude into the text. Once you've got a comfortable line length for the text, leave it alone. There's a very common practice, especially in magazines, of letting a picture or a bit of display type (such

Illustration in a two-column page layout: one with the image within the column (top), one with the image butting into both columns (above)

as a pull-quote) push into the text block from one side or another, forcing the text to wrap around the intruding shape. This can be done effectively, but most often it just means that for the depth of the intrusion, the text has to fit itself into a column that's too narrow, with the kinds of awkward spacing that you might expect. It's far better to design a multicolumn layout, and let the artwork or other display items occupy the width of a whole column (or several columns), rather than to vary the width of the text to accommodate the pretty pictures.

Being consistent

Whether your display type is a series of carefully modulated heads or a wild array of call-outs, banners, and thought balloons, you'll help your reader by treating the same kind of elements the same way throughout the book. Consistent treatment of related elements is essential for making the structure of the book clear to the reader — and for, most importantly, not misleading the reader.

Simplify the structure as much as possible, and use contrast to make it very clear what's what. That, along with good text typography, sums up the most important principles of designing a complex book.

No bells, no whistles

All too often, someone designing a book that's not complex, one that consists of nothing more than chapters of prose, tries to jazz it up by giving too much attention to elements that aren't important. The chapter opening is a good place to be a little flamboyant, but it's only there for the convenience of the reader; a flashy chapter-opening page that isn't easy to read, or that interrupts the reader and grabs the reader's attention, is a mistake.

One of the most annoying examples of misplaced creativity is overly elaborate page numbers, and running heads or running feet. (For simplicity's sake, I'll call them all "running heads" from now on, no matter where on the page they may fall.) The only purpose of the page number is to help the reader navigate; the same is true of a running head. (Though these days, there may be another use for the running head: so you can tell what book an excerpt came from when someone photocopies a few pages.) Fancy treatments of either page number or running head are self-defeating. They just get in the way. The information should be small and unobtrusive; it simply has to be there when the reader needs it.

References in the text
A variation of this has to do with notes and cross-references. How many times have you read a book that has endnotes (notes grouped in the back of the book, as opposed to footnotes on the same page), and been frustrated because it was hard to flip back and forth between the notes and the text without losing track of where you were? The information in the notes section that identifies what chapter the notes belong with ought to be the same information that you see on the page when you're reading the chapter. It doesn't do much good to see a section of notes in the back of the book labeled "Chapter Three" if the running heads in Chapter Three never mention the chapter number, identifying it only by chapter title.

If the book you're designing has cross-references, they should be obvious. In reference books, a traditional way of indicating names and terms that have their own entries is to put them in small caps — but this only works if the text face has a set of true small caps, and if the typesetter takes the trouble to letterspace them slightly looser than the surrounding text. Using the "small caps" command in a word-processing program to create fake small caps, by just shrinking the full caps, is a ghastly practice, which produces unreadable little blobs of tangled, too-light type.

If, on the other hand, you use italics to indicate either cross-references or something like words that have an entry in a glossary, make sure the italic of the typeface you're using is easily readable. (In general, Renaissance-style italics, such as Bembo italic or Minion italic, are easier to read than the rounded 19th-century Modern-style italics like Didot italic or Scotch italic. This is a rule of thumb with plenty of exceptions, of course.)

Once more with feeling

Once more with feeling

Front & back, inside & outside
In general, the front and back matter of a book (things like the table of contents, the preface, the index, and any appendices) should be in the style of the body of the book, but perhaps set in a smaller type size. The heart of any book is the main text, and everything else should grow out of that.

This applies even to the cover or dustjacket, although modern commercial publishing practice makes this extremely hard. The cover should be an outgrowth of the interior, ideally; at the very least, it has to harmonize with the design of the book itself. But in most large publishing companies, not only are the cover or jacket and the interior designed by two different people, but those people may not even be part of the same department or division.

Book covers and jackets are considered part of the marketing of the book, which is logical enough. But in a day when most books are paperbacks, where the cover is inextricably part of the book itself (unlike a removable jacket), this promotional material is going to be part of the book on the bookshelf, not just in the store. It had better be something attractive, something that a reader can bear to have on the shelf.

Incidentally, in a hardcover book with a jacket, the actual cover of the cloth binding should reflect the interior design, not the jacket design. It's rarely effective to use the same type treatment embossed into the cloth that you've used printed on the flimsy jacket. Similarly, there's no reason on earth for the book's title page to look like the cover.

Editors & designers

The last detail to cover is a philosophical one: which decisions are typographic and which are editorial. As someone who works as both an editor and a graphic designer, I find no conflict between these two ways of looking at text, but most people specialize in one or the other. Editors need to know what typographic tools they have at their disposal in order to make sense of complex information in a book, but they shouldn't be deciding how the designer will distinguish one kind of information from another. It's all too common, for instance, for an editor to insist that certain elements of the text should be in small caps, when the designer may find that the typeface doesn't have true small caps or that there's another, better way to handle the distinction needed.

Editors and designers need to talk to each other, all the way through the process of developing a book.

Resources

For all my present wordiness, this is just a quick once-over of some of the more obvious parts of designing a book. The best source is simply the books that you see every day — the best ones are the good examples, and the worst ones serve as warnings of what not to do.

There are a handful of very useful books on book design. Some of them were written before the desktop-publishing revolution, so they don't reflect current production techniques, but the best of them will give you a solid grounding in the principles involved — principles that don't change just because the type is set digitally these days. These are a few of the best books on the subject.

Jost Hochuli & Robin Kinross, *Designing Books: Practice and Theory*. (London: Hyphen Press, 1997.)

Jan Tschichold, *The Form of the Book: Essays on the Morality of Good Design*. (Vancouver, B.C., & Point Roberts, Wash.: Hartley & Marks, 1991.)

Adrian Wilson, *The Design of Books*. (New York: Reinhold Publishing Corporation, 1967. Reprinted with new introduction: San Francisco: Chronicle Books, 1993.)

Hugh Williamson, *Methods of Book Design: The Practice of an Industrial Craft*. (New Haven & London: Yale University Press, 1983. Third edition.)

Putting some spine into design

Nobody notices how the spines of book covers are designed, yet those are usually the first thing we see on a bookshelf.

[July 27, 2001]

MAYBE YOU CAN'T judge a book by its cover, but in a bookstore we judge most of them first by their spines. For most new books — not the ones lying out on tables or prominently displayed with their covers out, but the ones lining the shelves — the spine is all we see. The beautiful, dramatic cover, upon which great effort and sometimes even expense may have been lavished, never gets seen if a browsing bookbuyer doesn't reach out and pull the book off the shelf to take a look.

You might expect, given this cruel dynamic of the marketplace, that book publishers, and the designers of dustjackets and paperback covers for those publishers, would devote a lot of attention to what the spine looks like. But it seems to be the rare designer who gives the question much thought at all.

The spine of this comprehensive Italian dictionary from 1949 is striking and easy to read when the book is standing up, and stands out even on its side.

Standing up and standing out

As a book designer who is also a bookbuyer and a reader, I've thought about this a lot — and in the course of my professional life I've been able to put some of my thoughts into action. I know that when I scan the shelves of my favorite bookstores, it's the simplest, most dramatic, and most legible book spines that stand out.

Obviously, since most books are shelved vertically, the ideal direction for the type on the spine is horizontal, so that the words are the right way up when viewed by the browser's eye. And if the book is fat, the spine is wider and there's more space for the designer to work with. Sometimes the designer can use some of that space to frame the title and the author's name.

But few books are thick enough to allow this kind of spacious display. In most cases, the type is turned at right angles to the viewer's eye, in order to run along the vertical spine. In North America, the normal direction is from top to bottom; in Europe, it's usually bottom to top. (This means that in North America, in a pile of books stacked face up, all the titles are easy to read; in Europe, it's the pile of books stacked face down, with no front covers visible at all, where the titles on the spines are easy to read. Two different logics. The biggest practical effect is that readers browsing the shelves in a European bookstore crick their necks to the left, while those in North America crick theirs to the right.)

Since the type is not aligned with the way we see, it has to be even clearer than it would otherwise have to be. Crowded, cramped type gets lost in the clutter. No matter what the front cover looks like, capital letters make the best use of the narrow spine (no ascenders or descenders to extrude into the limited space). A little extra space between the letters — even more than you'd give them in a horizontal line — helps them stand out and be read.

Crisp letterforms (in this case, Big Caslon caps), if they're not too cramped, can stand out even when they fill the space on the spine.

DAVID LEE · MY TOWN

Clarity in complexity

Most of what I'm going to show is my own work, since that's easiest and perhaps most honest. But one example I'd like to include is the spine of a trade paperback edition of *Virtual Unrealities*, a collection of short stories by science-fiction writer Alfred Bester (published by Vintage Books). The designer, Evan Gaffney, uses the space in a unique way. The intrusions of amorphous blue photographic details in strict rectangles, and the swirling clock-face image, reflect the design of the front cover (and the back); they also tie this book in with others in the uniform series of Bester reprints, each of which features a different dominant color. The complexity of this spine draws a browser's eye in; the well-spaced type of the author's name and the title make it clear what this is. (Even the letterspacing of the subtitle, in caps and lowercase — which would normally not be a good idea — works here, given the size and the vertical nature of the spine.)

Clear typography within a complex composition is hard to pull off, but it works on this Vintage paperback.

Clarity and simplicity tend to stand out and be effective. But which element is most important? Which should be emphasized? You have to think about what will catch the browser's eye — the title, the name of the author, the publisher's logo, or something else entirely. In the case of the Alfred Bester book, it's Bester's name that will sell the book; he's known as one of the classic writers of science fiction. In the case of a book I designed for the University of Washington Press, *Answering Chief Seattle*, by Albert Furtwangler, the author's name was not well known, but the subject — Chief Seattle — is famous in the Pacific Northwest, and a title like *Answering Chief Seattle* ought to pique the intended reader's interest. So, in my design, the title is what stands out.

If the title is what's important, emphasize it.

FURTWANGLER **ANSWERING CHIEF SEATTLE** ▰

Using space

In one of my early book designs, a sequence of poetic prose by Sam Hamill about following in the footsteps of the haiku master Basho (published by Broken Moon

Press), my cover design was bold and simple, but on the spine I was timid, and I hadn't thought enough about what a book spine had to do. I chose very small type, and set it within the empty space of the spine. The type got lost there, rather than standing out against its ground.

BASHŌ'S GHOST   Sam Hamill   Broken Moon Press

Years later, in a volume of collected poems for White Pine Press, I got to give Sam Hamill a much more inviting spine. I knew that some readers of poetry would seek out books by Hamill, so his name had to stand out; but I also wanted to attract others, so the most striking emphasis (white type on a dark blue background) was given over to the intriguing title, *Destination Zero*.

HAMILL · DESTINATION ZERO

Sometimes neither the author's name nor the book's title is a guaranteed reader magnet. Poet Arthur Sze is well respected among certain circles of poetry readers, but he's hardly a household name. And the title of this book for Copper Canyon Press, *The Redshifting Web*, is a particularly awkward combination of words to do anything with on a book cover or spine. But I had an attractive piece of artwork that lent itself to being wrapped around from the front cover onto the spine, giving a natural division to the area of the spine. So instead of running a simple author/title line down a blank spine, I chose to blow up Sze's single-syllable last name large enough to dominate the top section, then I reduced the title until it fit within the artwork. The point was to be intriguing enough to make browsers stop and pull the book off the shelf.

SZE   THE REDSHIFTING WEB

Too colorful?

Color is an important factor in book spines, but contrast is a more important one. The most "typographic" colors are black and white, and I usually try to stick to those two for the type. The best second color is one that's light enough not to drown out black type, but dark enough that you can reverse out white type and still read it.

Sometimes using a color combination from the front cover, or even from the artwork, is effective. It's easy to get carried away, though. On the spine of Jane Miller's *Memory at These Speeds* (Copper Canyon), I made the mistake of using a blue for the author's name against a dark orangey-red, with a light yellowish orange for the title. The title stands out, but the blue and the red fight each other, in an electric effect, and Miller's name is hard to read.

JANE MILLER · MEMORY AT THESE SPEEDS

Spine space, the final frontier

Capital letters aren't the only possibility for a book spine. And even though italics, on a North American top-to-bottom spine, slant down, even farther away from the browser's horizontal orientation, sometimes they can be very effective. For Eleanor Wilner's collection *Reversing the Spell* (Copper Canyon), I thought the title itself would draw the most attention, so I made it prominent. The spine was wide enough that I could give the author's name horizontally, in contrast.

ELEANOR WILNER *Reversing the Spell*

The same technique of combining vertical and horizontal type worked on the spine of the first complete edition of Thomas McGrath's book-length poem, *Letter to an Imaginary Friend* (Copper Canyon). I probably played down McGrath's name too much (I should have used a contrasting or complementary typeface that was stronger, for his name), but the title stands out (the small caps are not faked; the typeface actually has "small caps" that are nearly as tall as the capital letters) and the spine was wide enough that I could use a cropped version of the very personal, very inviting photo of the author. You don't often get to use a person's face on a book spine.

The opposite problem comes when you've got a very narrow spine, for a very thin book. Heather Allen's *Leaving a Shadow* was one of the shortest books I've ever designed, an almost archetypal "slim volume of poems" (again, for Copper Canyon Press). The cover was a duotone, in black and silver, of a photograph with type against it. On the spine, there was no room for anything fancy; I simply used all the space, and all the variations at my disposal, setting the author's name in black and the title in white, both in letterspaced caps in a crisp typeface, against a pure silver background.

HEATHER ALLEN · LEAVING A SHADOW

Details, details
Why spend so much time thinking about a subject that almost no one, including book designers, gives much thought to? Because this, like so many neglected details of design, actually has a big impact on which items in the marketplace get noticed, and then bought. The spines of books ought to be pleasing, so that bookbuyers can stand to have them on their shelves once they've read them; but the first thing a book's spine has to do, in the real world, is attract that reader.

By focusing on this, I've been trying to deliver a small wake-up call to book designers and publishers, and also to shed a little light, for readers, on something that affects them daily but that they've probably never really noticed. Design really is everywhere.

design & culture

Detail from the cover of INSCRIPTIONS, *with part of a rubbing of one of the actual inscriptions in a second color.*

Typography, architecture, & inscriptions

An elegant book edited and designed by Jack Stauffacher shows how the inscriptions from San Francisco's old downtown library carry on the traditions of Western learning displayed on public architecture.

[*March 24, 2003*]

"IN THE MIDST of change, civic buildings remain as central icons of our community. This book is about these civic icons and their often compromised survival." — *Jack Stauffacher*

Jack Stauffacher is a highly respected printer and typographer, proprietor of the Greenwood Press in San Francisco for more than 60 years, and a friend of the continuity of culture across the centuries. The book he has put together, *Inscriptions* (published jointly by the Book Club of California and the San Francisco Public Library), documents the public inscriptions that adorned the Old Main Library — the SFPL's former home in a Beaux-Arts building that opened in 1917 and formed part of the city's ornate post-earthquake Civic Center. The main library moved into a brand-new building across the street several years ago, and the Old Main was in the process of being converted into a new home for the San Francisco Asian Art Museum.

There was great controversy about what to do with the series of murals depicting California coastal scenes that had decorated the interior walls of the central staircase of the old building, but in the fracas hardly any attention was paid to the panels of inscriptions that ran in a frieze above those murals. As Old Main partisans recalled, those inscriptions and those murals had formed an essential part of the public experience of using the library for most of the 20th century. And what is more essential to the spirit of a library than thoughtful words?

The central staircase and colonnade of the Old Main Library, with murals and inscriptions around the walls.

"Dr. Taylor selected terse maxims from the canon of Western literature for frieze panels and lintels around the second floor colonnade," writes historian Gray Brechin in the book's primary essay. "These apothegms served as guideposts from the past, a compendium of sage advice on how to lead a fulfilling and civilized life as one strove toward the light." The "Dr. Taylor" that Brechin mentions was Edward Robeson Taylor, "physician, lawyer, printer, poet, and former mayor," who not only chose the texts for all the inscriptions but was one of the driving forces behind the building's creation.

Brechin's essay places the San Francisco library in the context of other great public libraries in the Beaux-Arts style, from the Bibliothèque Sainte-Geneviève in Paris, designed by Henri Labrouste in the 1830s, through the Boston Public Library, to the American West Coast.

"Impressive as it was," Brechin points out, "Labrouste's library was but one building in the capital city and thus not easily accessible to most French citizens who lived far from Paris. It remained for advocates in the United States to popularize learning in a manner commensurate with Thomas Jefferson's belief that a lasting democracy depends upon widespread and continuing education." Brechin gives a thorough survey of how public libraries came to cities like San Francisco, and how they got the distinctive architectural styles they have. This is a context for the focus of the book: the inscriptions.

Photographing in the shadows
Complementing Brechin's essay is a series of photographs taken by San Francisco photographer Dennis Letbetter, on a hurried tour with Stauffacher and others through the already-closed Old Main in 1997, of each of the inscriptions *in situ*. (He also took photos of the library's interior, and later of related library buildings in other cities.) In his own "Note on Photographing the

Another of the inscriptions from the central hall.

Inscriptions," Letbetter says, "Andrea Grimes led me to each inscription, one after the other, accompanied by a pressing and begrudging security escort. Everything had to happen in a very limited time, and there was even some suggestion that I might not be allowed enough time to finish my work. Lights were either completely burned out, uneven, or nonexistent. The inscriptions themselves had acquired a somber patina from age as well as from those more tolerant years when smoking was allowed on the grand staircase — evidence of the neglect that the city allowed the great Beaux-Arts structure to suffer."

Grimes herself, Special Collections Librarian at SFPL, writes: "My second memory of that afternoon was the look on Jack's face as we emerged into the light. I think this was his defining moment. Questions and ideas were taking shape that would become the subject of years of research, conversations, meetings, and proposals. Jack was unclear about the destiny of the inscriptions. What would happen to them during the building's restoration? Would they remain intact where they were originally placed by anonymous craftsmen in 1916?" (In the event, they were cleaned and restored.) "Would anyone know why these inscriptions were here or what they had meant in a different time? For my part, I wondered who wrote the words and how they were selected long ago."

A one-line inscription from the library.

Researching the sources of the quotations was one of the major tasks behind this book; in the end, all but two were identified. (Taylor left no record of who he was quoting, and he may have modified the wording here and there to fit the space.) "One of the most exhaustingly difficult quotations, 'Handle a book as a bee does a flower, extract its sweets but do not injure it,' was cause for

Michael Harvey examining one of the inscription panels.

One of the inscriptions from the library's central hall, cast in faux-travertine.

celebration after its accidental discovery," says Grimes. Frustratingly, she doesn't say how the source (Charles Caleb Colton) was finally found.

Context and the long view
Besides the main tale of the library and its inscriptions, the book includes several supplementary essays that put this specific, local story into a larger context that reaches all the way back through the history of Western civilization.

Michael Harvey, known for his carving of inscriptions in stone on public buildings like the Sainsbury Wing of the National Gallery in London, flew to San Francisco to examine the SFPL inscriptions and explain how they had been created. "We have to go back to Roman practice to understand how inscriptions were created then," he says, "and how little in essence these methods have changed in succeeding centuries… It was rare for a shop to specialize in inscriptions; these were generally carried out in shops equipped for general stonework. In essence, this is what happened in 1915, when the San Francisco library's inscriptions were planned." He shows how they were done using letter patterns, and cast rather than individually carved, in a newly developed faux-travertine that recalled the surfaces of public buildings in ancient Rome.

Type designer Sumner Stone, who has given lectures on Roman inscriptions, contributes "Rock Wraps Paper," about the phenomenon of public lettering, its permanence, and the letterforms used. "There is much to be said for physical presence," writes Stone. "What would we be reading today had it not been for the remains of imperial Roman inscriptions in the landscape of the Italian humanists?"

Stauffacher adds a short, impassioned postscript, and also includes a translation of the relevant section from Leon Battista Alberti's 15th-century treatise on architecture, a section called "Of the Inscriptions and Symbols

Detail of a page spread from the book, showing examples of other kinds of inscriptions in stone, from various eras.

Carved on Sepulchres." The inscriptions that Alberti himself designed for his buildings in Renaissance Italy, says Stauffacher, "are remarkable for their insightful clarity and perfect integration with his many architectural works." *Inscriptions* is all about this integration of words and buildings, and the place of both in a community.

A handy paper monument
The book is beautifully designed and produced, as might be expected from a master printer with a talented team of contributors. (Stauffacher had to be persuaded to list himself as editor, and not just run his own name in with the other bylines.) On the cover, over a full-size detail of a rubbing from one of the inscriptions, runs the simple title, "Inscriptions"; inside, on the title page, this is supplemented with a subtitle: "at the Old Public Library of San Francisco." The format is almost square (9½ × 11), which gives ample room to display photographs and present the text in an understated two-column format (using Sumner Stone's Cycles, an elegant typeface that seems both calligraphic and lapidary). Stauffacher's book design is always deceptively simple, and very comfortable to read. The physical book, printed on silky-textured Mohawk Superfine, feels good in the hand, though such a wide book might be more comfortable to hold if it were hardcover rather than soft.

What lasts
At the end of his essay, Sumner Stone asks, "Will these inscriptions of the Old Main Library still be decipherable in 2,000 years? Will their cultural context be understood by the epigrapher of the future? Will they outlast this book? Will their Roman letters endure another two millennia, carefully studied by students of the lettering arts?" These are questions that only time can answer, but both the inscriptions and this book were made to last.

Close-up of a piece of wooden type and part of an 18th-century edition of Vico's SCIENZA NUOVA.

The Vico collaboration

Wooden and metal type are at the heart of two paired portfolios of images — one letterpress, one photographic — inspired by the 18th-century philosopher Giambattista Vico.

[December 10, 2003]

One of the new prints created by Jack Stauffacher using huge wooden type in abstract ways.

Dennis Letbetter's close-up photograph of a piece of 7-point type held by Jack Stauffacher.

AN UNUSUAL COLLABORATION has come to fruition in San Francisco. It's the work of a master printer, Jack Stauffacher, and a fine photographer, Dennis Letbetter — inspired by an 18th-century book by the Neapolitan philosopher Giambattista Vico, and focused on the stuff and substance of typography.

I've written about Jack Stauffacher before, including a column about his use of huge wooden type to create letterpress prints that are intended as art rather than typography. For this new project, inspired by the artfully philosophical prose of Vico, Stauffacher has created a new series of prints, which incorporate not only the huge wooden letter-shapes but also small lines of text, phrases extracted from Vico's *Scienza Nuova* ("New Science") and hand-set in text type: little words among the giants. These limited-edition prints make up one of the two portfolios of the Vico project.

The other portfolio is photographic. Dennis Letbetter, who has collaborated with Stauffacher before, took a series of macro-photographs, those extreme close-ups that capture the finest details of small objects and make them seem huge and out of scale. The subjects of Letbetter's photos were the objects of printing: individual pieces of metal type, by themselves and composed into lines and blocks of text; letterpress ink and the patterns it makes; and details of the printing and construction of the original editions of Vico's book itself. These photographs zoom in on the physical reality of print and type in a way that few other images have.

Prints by Stauffacher and Letbetter on display at the Bonnafont Gallery in San Francisco.

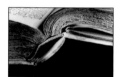

Binding of an original edition of Vico's book, photographed in extreme close-up by Dennis Letbetter.

Connecting the arts

The results of this collaboration were first on view at an opening at the Bonnafont Gallery in San Francisco, which celebrated the connections and interconnections of art, craft, philosophy, and a great variety of people.

Prints hung on the walls, and in a couple of clear-topped display cases were artifacts of Vico and of printing: the hand-tied block of 7-point type, for instance, that features in one of Letbetter's photos, and a copy of the miniature third edition of Vico's work, which used type of this infinitesimal size on pages that would fit into a small pocket. (Stauffacher had set this block of type himself just to find out what it would feel like to set such tiny type, and imagine what might have been involved in setting an entire book in it by hand.)

Enthusiasm

In a short public presentation during the opening, Stauffacher spoke about the importance of Giambattista Vico (saying that he wasn't going to explain anything about Vico's thinking: "You'll just have to go read the book yourselves!") and the oblique way in which it had inspired both him and Letbetter in their respective work. Then he asked Pino Trogu, an Italian graphic designer who lives in San Francisco, to read aloud the passage in Italian from Vico's original text that Jack had used as a sample; and he asked me, since I had come in from out of town, to read the English translation. (We both had to incorporate a few phrases of Latin, too.) The real meat of the evening was probably Jack's informal expositions in front of a few attentive people in the midst of the party. There is nothing like Jack Stauffacher on a roll, explaining the craft of something he loves.

He had had a chance to do this in front of a much bigger audience a couple of months before, when he was one of the featured speakers at the AIGA's annual conference, in Vancouver. He showed some of the prints that would

Jack Stauffacher explaining the tactile pleasures of creating art out of huge wooden type.

Jack Stauffacher and young designers at the AIGA national conference in Vancouver.

make up the Vico portfolio, along with the literary books that have made him respected as a printer. His animated explanations captivated the young designers crowding around him.

Up close and material

Some of Letbetter's intensely focused black-and-white photos have the quality of 19th-century photography; one view of a single line of composed metal type, shot from the side from only inches away, looks like it might be an early photo of the chimneypots of Paris. When you realize what it really is, it changes your perspective on type and typography, quite literally.

Stauffacher's subtle bending of the crafts of inking and printing to get specific visual effects, and his arrangement of the gigantic letters and parts of letters, create abstract images that aren't just shape and color but physical, tactile interactions of the materials of paper, ink, and type.

This sort of artistic creation is far from the practical exigencies of job printing, or the deadlines and pressures of commercial typography, but it is a unique joining of several pragmatic crafts and the highest aspirations of human thinking.

The Parmenides Project

Can a pre-Socratic philosopher be brought back to life through hand printing and cutting new metal type in the 21st century?

[*June 15, 2001*]

The FRAGMENTS *of Parmenides, published by Peter Koch in 2004.*

PARMENIDES OF ELEA doesn't get a lot of press these days. He was a 6th century BC Greek philosopher, one of what we call the pre-Socratics (he flourished a century and a half before Socrates), and his surviving work is a collection of fragments of his single long poem. (Or it might have been a medium-size poem. Since all we have is fragments, how can we know?) The subject of his poem isn't adventure or war or a love story; it's the fundamental question of being and non-being.

Berkeley printer and publisher Peter Rutledge Koch decided several years ago that Parmenides was worthy of a new edition. (Koch specializes in ambitious hand-printed books and digital/letterpress collaborations; a taste of his serious but un-solemn approach might be seen in the title of the catalog of his work published in 1995 by the New York and San Francisco public libraries: *Peter Koch Printer, Surrealist Cowboys, Maverick Poets and Pre-Socratic Philosophers*.) He commissioned poet/typographer Robert Bringhurst to make a new translation, into idiomatic North American English, and asked first stonecutter Christopher Stinehour and then punchcutter Dan Carr to create a wholly new Greek typeface for the project — in metal, for hand setting.

The resulting book, with English and Greek texts printed on facing pages, will be a monument of scholarship and booksmanship, but it has yet to see the light of day. [*It was finally published in 2004.*] What did burst onto the scene last Sunday and Monday in San Francisco, at the Koret Auditorium in the main San Francisco Public Library, was a symposium, a presentation by the collabo-

rators, called "The Parmenides Project: The Hand & the Computer in an Early Twenty-first Century Book."

Peter Koch introduced the event and acted as master of ceremonies for the four talks and one reading spread over a day and a half in downtown San Francisco. On Sunday, Koch gave an introduction to the whole project, followed by Christopher Stinehour on the art of cutting letters in stone and drawing on the computer. The next day, Robert Bringhurst explained the context of Parmenides and the language in which he wrote (including the sound of ancient Greek, which we can reconstruct up to a point because the Greeks themselves wrote so much about the subject); Bringhurst's ability to bring an entire cultural tradition to bear on a single question brings ideas and language alive. Then Dan Carr explained, and demonstrated, the nature of hand-cutting metal type punches and its relation to digital type design. Finally, to bring it all back to the heart of the matter, Bringhurst delivered a dramatic, impassioned reading of his translation of the fragments of Parmenides.

A new old type

Although the English translation will be typeset in an existing typeface (16pt Van Dijck, in the sample just printed), Koch was looking for a typeface for the Greek original that looked like Greek letters cut in stone or on metal coins in the 6th century BC — a sort of "refined primitive," as he said. Christopher Stinehour had already created a typeface for an earlier book of Diogenes based on ancient Greek graffiti — the notes, slogans, and admonitions scrawled on walls and bits of metal or pots in ancient Athens. Stinehour's Diogenes typeface came out monoline, simple, and informal, like the lettering of the graffiti. He refined this when he began thinking about Parmenides, looking at inscriptional forms — carved, rather than scrawled or scratched — and trying out a very geometric model, made up almost entirely of circles and straight lines.

Robert Bringhurst drew sketches of all the characters that would be needed to print Parmenides: twenty-four characters, plus variants and punctuation. Stinehour made "lots of drawings" of letters from various inscriptions, simple drawings with a felt-tip pen. He scanned these drawings into Adobe Illustrator, then drew over the scans in Illustrator to create the outlines, which he then imported into Fontographer to turn them into a font.

Dan Carr designed the typeface for the Ancient Greek text to resemble ancient inscriptional forms.

Although what Stinehour created was used as a prototype for the project, Koch commissioned Dan Carr to create the final typeface for Parmenides and to cut the punches from which the metal type will be cast. Carr took his inspiration from the archaic writing of the 6th century and earlier—what he called a "more contrapuntal or organic letterform" than the geometric forms found in later centuries.

Dan Carr is one of a handful of working punchcutters in the world. He demonstrated what it was like to cut punches, with tiny files and gravers and other specialized implements, peering closely at the little piece of metal as he shaped its end. To work at such a small size, it's necessary to use a magnifying glass, though Carr would periodically check what he was doing by making a "smoke proof" (literally holding the piece of metal in the smoke from a candle flame to pick up a coating of soot, then pressing the soot-blackened end onto a piece of paper to produce an image).

Hands on
The odd set-up on stage—of overhead lights and a vertically suspended camera and a big table covered

Dan Carr carving a punch (top), and some of the punches carved for the Parmenides project (above).

with stone-carver's tools — came into its own as Christopher Stinehour moved from his lecture to an actual demonstration of the art of cutting letters in stone. The suspended camera gave us an overhead view of his workspace, which was projected onto the screen, so we could see his hands and the tools and the stone as he worked. (Occasionally he'd get carried away and get his head in front of the camera, or the stone would shift out of the visual frame, but he'd keep correcting for this so we could watch him.) You could see the enlarged view of the slate or limestone (he used both) being cut into as Stinehour's hammer knocked his chisel, or you could shift your gaze from the screen to the man onstage, hammering away carefully but quickly on the stone in front of him, and the puffs of white stone dust spurting into the air with every blow.

The next day, punchcutter Dan Carr used the same set-up to demonstrate how he cuts a metal punch — the little stick of metal with a tiny, letter-sized face on the end in the shape of a single letter (in reverse), which letter casters use to make the metal matrix from which the piece of type itself will be cast.

Seeing these two centuries-old, hands-on processes going on right in front of us made them seem accessible, like something that any of us could do if only we took the trouble to learn how. (Where's my hammer and chisel?)

Do it again

This was no sterile intellectual exercise. Although Parmenides is considered to be "hard," Peter Koch and his collaborators have devoted their efforts to this project because Parmenides' words speak to them, and they want those words to speak to others in the future.

The most amazing parts of the two-day seminar were the two live demonstrations of physical letter-cutting, and Bringhurst's heartfelt, resonant reading of his translation of the fragments themselves. These are events that will never fit between the covers of a book. But perhaps this will not be the only time they are done in public. Koch spoke, at least theoretically, of doing this again in New York or London or Berlin.

Type goes global

A multilingual exhibition of the best contemporary type designs went on public display at United Nations headquarters in New York City.

[*January 27, 2003*]

ON JANUARY 17, 2003, a bitterly cold evening in New York, the *bukva:raz!* exhibition opened in the visitors' gallery at the headquarters of the United Nations. The opening was attended by around 200 people, who braved the cold and the after-hours UN security system to see the first showing of *bukva:raz!* in North America.

The salient points about *bukva:raz!* are that it was an international competition organized by ATypI (Association Typographique Internationale) to encourage excellence in the design of typefaces for all languages and writing systems around the world, and that it was ATypI's contribution to the United Nations Year of Dialogue among Civilizations (2001).

The idea for the competition was hatched by two Russians, Maxim Zhukov and Vladimir Yefimov. Maxim works as a typographic advisor to the UN in New York, so he was uniquely positioned to make the connection between the typographic community and the world political organization. And the event had clear support from the UN: not only did they agree to hold the exhibition in their exhibit space in the classic Modernist UN headquarters building, but the opening was jointly hosted by Mark Batty, president of ATypI, and Giandomenico Picco, the Personal Representative of the Secretary-General for the United Nations Year of Dialogue among Civilizations.

Live in New York
The formal part of the opening was quite brief. Gillian Sorensen, Assistant Secretary-General for External Relations, welcomed the guests and did the introductions.

*Speakers Gary Van Dis,
Mark Batty, Joachim
Müller-Lancé, and Gian-
domenico Picco before the
opening ceremony.*

*Attendees viewing the type
showings during the opening.*

Giandomenico Picco set the stage by reminding us what the Year of Dialogue really means, in a short poetic statement ("Are there children of a lesser God? / Are there lives which are less worth? / Are there truths which are more so?"), putting the concerns of type designers into the wider context of global peace and war. Mark Batty described the project and thanked the sponsors. Gary Van Dis, Vice President Corporate Creative Director at Condé Nast (whose major sponsorship had made the exhibition possible), spoke of how typography fosters communication in his business of international publishing. Joachim Müller-Lancé, who had four winning typefaces in the show, spoke for the many type designers represented. Finally, Gillian Sorensen invited the speakers to join Giandomenico Picco in cutting a symbolic ribbon (spanning two upright stanchions in front of the exhibit) and declaring the exhibition open.

Joachim Müller-Lancé, who had come in from San Francisco, was both funny and poignant when he spoke. He described the lonely work of the type designer and the odd economics of the business, then he too put it into a broader context: "We all know," he said, "the serious developments and events of the past months. Gaps have opened, and we need to build bridges in talking and writing. As type designers, we hope to provide the nuts and bolts for these bridges. Doors have been closed, so new windows have to be opened. We hope we can be the hinges."

Laetitia Wolff had curated the exhibition and made sure it actually got set up in time for the opening. It looked impressive, especially in that setting. The panels showing the 100 winning typefaces were hung on a set of freshly painted movable walls in the exhibit area beyond the visitors' information desk. Besides the typeface showings (of intimate interest to everyone involved in the type business), Maxim had designed seven full-length panels showing examples of seven different writing systems,

Joachim Müller-Lancé annotating the panel that used one of his winning typefaces to show Japanese kanji.

with a word on each set in one of the winning typefaces; these were in white and black against the competition's signature bright red.

One of the seven panels, the one showing Japanese, used Joachim's typeface Shirokuro to set the word *ai* ("love") in kanji. After the formal ceremony, Joachim annotated the panel, using a large marker to write in three more words in Japanese ("mind," "heart," and "hands") and contribute a unique bilingual gloss to the prepared display. (He had almost as many people observing this action as had listened to the earlier ceremony.)

Light in a cold world

After the opening proper, many of the guests walked several blocks up First Avenue (against a stiff wind) to have drinks and dinner at Meltemi, a Greek restaurant that Maxim had suggested. It wasn't a long walk at all, but by the time we got there, we were all feeling like frozen popsicles. (Fiona Ross, who had been on the jury when the competition was judged last winter in Moscow, and who was in New York as a judge of the current Type Directors Club competition, said that it was colder that night in New York than it was in Moscow. "I know," she said. "I just checked.")

I don't describe all this just to document a social event. The importance of the *bukva:raz!* exhibit at the United Nations is its role as a small but crucial contribution to — precisely — dialogue among civilizations. The making of those nuts and bolts and hinges, as Joachim Müller-Lancé aptly put it, is important work. The best way we have of countering the destructive forces at work in the world today is to go on creating, and to encourage clearer and better communication. We aren't just talking to ourselves.

Zapfest

Gudrun and Hermann Zapf

Zapfest, held in San Francisco in September and October 2001, celebrated the confluence of digital type and the calligraphic tradition. Honoring Hermann and Gudrun Zapf, the exhibition and its concurrent series of lectures was a seminal event for both calligraphers and typographers worldwide.

[*April/September, 2001*]

UNDERLYING all of the pixelized letterforms we see on the screen or the page is a long tradition of handwritten letters. Some of our digital fonts are more directly influenced by calligraphy than others; in many cases, it's the liveliness imbued by the traces of the pen that gives a typeface its distinctive sparkle.

Two of the finest practitioners of both traditional calligraphy and modern digital type design are Hermann Zapf and Gudrun Zapf von Hesse. Virtually everyone who works on a computer and prints anything from it is familiar with some of Hermann Zapf's work, whether they know it or not. His 1949 typeface Palatino has become one of the ubiquitous default fonts on laser printers, although it has undergone some modification in the passage from metal to PostScript. And of course the eponymous Zapf Chancery — or at least one of its several variants — is on pretty much everybody's machine. Although Gudrun Zapf has been a less prolific type designer than her husband, her Nofret type family and its predecessor Diotima have been widely used by discerning designers.

They have consistently embraced new technology and turned it to the service of enduring quality. At the beginning of September 2001, in San Francisco, an exhibition opened and a series of ancillary events began, to highlight this connection and the fruits of their efforts. The exhibition was officially called "Calligraphic Type Design

Palatino ABCDEFGHIJKLMN
OPQRSTUVWXYZ & 1234567890
abcdefghijklmnopqrstuvwxyz

›MICHELANGELO‹ABC
DEFGHIJKLMNOPQRSTUV
WXYZ & KQR ✠ 1234567890

ABCDEFGH
IJKLMNOPQR
STUVWXYZ
abcdefghijklmnopqrstuvwxyz

Three typefaces designed by Hermann Zapf: Palatino (top), Michelangelo (middle), Zapfino (bottom)

in the Digital Age: An Exhibition in Honor of the Contributions of Hermann and Gudrun Zapf"; informally, it's being referred to as Zapfest.

Who, what, where

There is a large and flourishing community of calligraphers and lovers of the calligraphic hand in Northern California (as elsewhere); Zapfest grew out of the enthusiasm of a local society called the Friends of Calligraphy, though it involves quite a few other groups besides the hard-core community of scribes. The three curators of the exhibition were Sumner Stone, the noted American type designer; Susie Taylor, curator of the Harrison Collection at the San Francisco Public Library; and Linnea Lundquist, typographer, calligrapher, type designer, and former student of Hermann Zapf's.

Transcending the medium

It takes a great deal of skill and painstaking work to turn written letters – whether casual handwriting or formal calligraphy – into a typeface. The subtle modulations that you'd make each time you write a letter have to be generalized into something that will work when it's repeated hundreds of time in dozens of combinations. Both Hermann and Gudrun Zapf are masters of this.

Perhaps the most ambitious attempt to translate calligraphic exuberance into typographic form is Hermann Zapf's typeface Zapfino, which he produced with Gino Lee. Zapfino features an amazing variety of swashes, combinations, and alternate forms, which a sensitive typographer can use to re-create some of the hand-drawn effect of original calligraphy. (Of course, if original calligraphy is what you need, you should hire a calligrapher.)

Any typeface that tries to reproduce calligraphy is a compromise; the question is whether it works well on its own terms. But ordinary type that retains the movement

abcdefghijklmnopqrstuvwxyz
ABCDEFGHIJKLMNOPQRSTUVW
XYZ · abcdefghijklmnopqrst
uvwxyz · ABCDEFGHIJKLMN
OPQRSTUVWXYZ · abcdefghi
jklmnopqrstuvwxyz · ABCDEF
GHIJKLMNOPQRSTUVWXYZ

THE QUICK BROWN FOX
jumps over the lazy dog
The quick brown fox jumps

Two typefaces designed by Gudrun Zapf: Nofret (top), Columbine (bottom)

of the pen in its strokes and curves — that has been a goal of type designers for centuries.

Gudrun's work

Gudrun Zapf von Hesse is less well known than her prolific husband Hermann, but she was already a calligrapher and book-binder when they met at an exhibit in the late 1930s. (As Hermann later put it, he "married the competition.") Her first typeface, Diotima, was commissioned by D. Stempel AG, the type foundry that employed Hermann.

Gudrun's slide presentation showed exquisite examples of her book bindings, often in leather with gold foil stamping, many times using types that she had developed specifically for this purpose, and many samples of her gorgeous calligraphy. Smoke proofs of Diotima (a quick way of proofing the work of cutting metal type punches) gave way to such unusual images as two magazine ads for Opel automobiles from the 1980s, using the fine-boned Diotima as the typeface for the headlines.

Among her other notable typefaces, the Nofret family (1986) was originally going to be called Diotima Book. The resemblance in the lighter weights in obvious; the italics are especially similar, but Nofret's roman is narrower than Diotima's extremely spacious characters — more of a text face. Gudrun expanded Nofret in the direction of very heavy weights, too, which take on a massive sparkle found in very few bold typefaces.

Her examples of type and calligraphy in use were sometimes breathtaking. Even as a slide projected onto a slightly overlit screen, her setting of the preamble of the United Nations charter, blind stamped into dampened paper, was beautiful. The watercolors she showed from more recent years melded the forms of letters with the interplay of blocks of color. A page from a booklet from 1955 that I'd like to study in more detail, showing inter-

Grief
Sweat

Jody Aliesan

*A book cover using a digital
form of Gudrun Zapf's
typeface Diotima.*

leaved lines of black, swash-filled civilité lettering and roman, demonstrated her mastery of contrast.

Although Gudrun doesn't speak English as fluently as Hermann, and perhaps didn't give us as much detailed commentary as she might have if she'd been speaking her native language, the audience was delighted to see the work and hear from its source. Both Gudrun and Hermann are quiet, soft-spoken, and reserved, without flamboyance or pretension. Their work speaks for them. If Hermann has come to cast a very long shadow, through his prominence in the world of type, Gudrun shows no signs of letting her own shadow be lost in his; and this exhibition and her talk may remind us what a talented artist and craftswoman she is and what a body of work she has created. I wouldn't be surprised to see this event inspire a number of graphic designers to put Gudrun's typefaces to use more often in the coming years.

The other half

Among those who are familiar with the art and craft of type, Hermann Zapf is known as a master of three different forms: calligraphy, the design of typefaces, and the design of books. His work has been collected and shown off in several fine books and catalogs in the course of his career, but these have a tendency to sell out quickly and become rare and expensive. Now the full range of his work is available on a CD-ROM, whose design and production was overseen by Zapf himself: *The world of alphabets by Hermann Zapf: A kaleidoscope of drawings and letterforms.*

The CD-ROM illustrates 200 of Zapf's works, and it's orchestrated with music and a little animation so that you can navigate through it any way you like — browsing and rambling or following the defined course of a chronological presentation. For the talk in San Francisco, Zapf followed his own chronology, but he moved through it quickly, supplying the commentary with his own voice-

The CD-ROM of Hermann Zapf's life and work.

over rather than waiting for the captions to appear under the images on screen. ("Going through the whole thing," he said, " would otherwise take a couple of hours.")

A portrait of the artist

The most fascinating things for those of us familiar with his work were the early pieces and the bits of biography. Hermann Zapf was born in Nuremberg just three days before the armistice that ended World War 1. Nuremberg in 1918, he said, "was not a good place to come into the world": in addition to the aftermath of the war, there was revolution in Berlin and the devastating effects of the Spanish flu—which killed more people than the war did. Two of Hermann's siblings died in the epidemic, and as a newborn baby he himself was in poor health and not expected to live. ("As I'm about to turn 83," he told us, "I guess the doctors were wrong.")

You can see inklings of the talent to come in young Hermann's childhood attempts at writing decorative initial letters, and in the secret alphabet he created so his mother wouldn't be able to read his notes to his friends. One image shows some of the self-made toys he played with, since the family couldn't afford to buy toys from the shops. Perhaps most remarkable of these early efforts was the do-it-yourself electrical kit that Hermann put together in a neatly constructed box, complete with an illustrated manual of how to use it, written out entirely by hand.

The lure of letters

The electrical kit was no fluke; the young Zapf was a tinkerer, and he had intended to become an electrical engineer. But this was Germany in the 1930s. For political reasons (his father was active in the trade unions), Hermann wasn't allowed to study electrical engineering. Almost by accident, he became a photo retoucher ("I went home from the interview and looked up 'photo-retouching' in the encyclopedia"), which got him into the publishing and printing world. But it was a memorial exhibition of the lettering work of Rudolph Koch, who had died just a few years before, that captured the young man's imagination: "This changed my life." He would become a letterer.

He went to work for the Stempel type foundry, one of the most renowned in Germany, and ended up in charge of their typeface program. (It was in that capacity, after the war, that he met his future wife, Gudrun von Hesse; he saw her lettering and commissioned a typeface from it.) During World War II, he was a cartographer with the German army in France, making maps of Spain (which were never put to use). As a prisoner of war in a military hospital, he learned Arabic from some of the French African soldiers who were there with him. This knowledge came in handy when he later had to design an Arabic typeface, Alahram, for Stempel's export market in the 1950s.

The type designs of Zapf's that we now think of as "classic" — Palatino, Aldus, Melior, and Optima — were all done in the '50s, as were any number of others. On a trip to Italy he discovered the modulated strokes of the serif-less letters set into the floor of the church of Santa Croce in Florence. On the CD-ROM you can see the two 1000-lira Italian banknotes that Zapf used, for lack of any other paper in his pocket, to sketch out the first ideas for what developed into the typeface Optima, inspired by those letters on the floor.

Old friends
The following week, Jack Stauffacher, one of the pre-eminent letterpress printer/book-designers of San Francisco, kicked off the Zapfest lecture series in an onstage interview conducted by Sumner Stone, which began with a bit of raw film footage of Hermann Zapf in action that hadn't been seen since 1960.

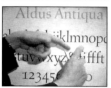

"Finger dancing": stills from film footage of Hermann Zapf (left) and Jack Stauffacher at the first U.S. exhibition of Zapf's work, in 1960.

This is your life

In keeping with the Zapfest theme, Stauffacher's talk focused on his time at Carnegie Institute of Technology (now Carnegie Mellon University), in Pittsburgh, in the late 1950s and early 1960s. Stauffacher had been able to bring Hermann Zapf over from Germany to lecture to the students at Carnegie — Zapf's first visit to the United States.

While Zapf was in Pittsburgh, Stauffacher put on an exhibition of Zapf's work, and a local television crew filmed him in a staged tour of the exhibition — walking through it with Stauffacher and others, explaining printed pieces and gesticulating expressively as he described the curves of the letterforms. (Stauffacher calls this "finger dancing," especially the part where the two of them, in their younger selves, are seen tracing arcs and serifs and stems, and it seems that Zapf is conducting a silent symphony of script.) The original TV broadcast has been lost, but fortuitously — just in time for Zapfest — Stauffacher unearthed the raw footage, unedited and without sound, along with a short piece of film he himself had made of Zapf teaching one of his classes. With the help of the San Francisco Public Library, he had these bits transferred to videotape, and ready to be shown when he mounted the stage at Koret Auditorium on September 8.

Hermann Zapf and Gudrun Zapf von Hesse, who had given their own presentations the week before and were still in San Francisco, were sitting in the audience, near the front. When Stauffacher announced that he had a little surprise, which he wanted us all to watch in silence, they had no idea what was coming. As the footage unrolled, I stole a glance at Hermann's face, just in time to see puzzlement starting to turn to amazement. Not only had he not seen this film footage in forty years, but he told Jack, afterward, that he had never seen it at all. It was a total surprise.

First proof of "Z-Antiqua"
(Hunt Roman), from the
book HUNT ROMAN: THE
BIRTH OF A TYPE.

Hunt Roman

While Zapf was at Carnegie, Stauffacher had the opportunity to persuade the Hunt Botanical Library there to
commission a unique typeface — cut in metal, for hand-
setting — just for the library's own publications, and to
invite Zapf to design it for them. He had the support of
the library's patron, Rachel McMasters Miller Hunt,
herself a master bookbinder and a champion of good
printing. The new typeface began life as "Z-Antiqua"
(there are sketches of it in the Zapfest exhibit), but it was
later given the name it's known by today: Hunt Roman.

A small, elegant book about it, *Hunt Roman: The Birth
of a Type*, was published by the Pittsburgh Bibliophiles in
1965, and copies can still sometimes be found. Although
this book uses Hunt Roman for its short text, the face
was intended as a display face, for use with Kis Janson as
the library's text face. (Stauffacher had been instrumental
in bringing an understanding of the work of Nicholas
Kis, the 17th-century Hungarian punchcutter whose
types were long misidentified as "Janson," to the modern
printing world.) Hunt Roman, which looks very much
like a Zapf roman typeface, with its chiseled lines and
its slightly squared curves, was cut only in 14pt, 18pt,
and 24pt sizes. It is still a proprietary face of the Hunt
Library; it has never been digitized (and Hermann Zapf
expressed his hope that it never would be).

A tradition's end

After presenting the surprise film, Stauffacher settled
down in an armchair onstage for Sumner Stone to interview him. They talked animatedly about the origins of
Hunt Roman, the unique circumstances under which
Stauffacher found himself at Carnegie with the opportunity to make such a project happen ("it was the will of the
gods; I could never have planned this"), and what made
that particular time and place special. Stauffacher said
that in retrospect he realized that he'd had an unparal-

leled opportunity to be in at the end of something: the 500-year tradition of metal type. Although Hunt Roman was not the last new typeface cut in metal for hand-set-ting, it was nearly the last; certainly it must have been one of the last created for commercial use (if a proprietary typeface for a botanical library can be called commercial). Shortly after that, as Stauffacher pointed out, everything changed; the world he was lecturing in last month was a world of digital fonts, where letterpress printing and hand-set type are the realm of the individual craftsman and craftswoman, not part of the general tide of mass publishing.

Of course, as a printer and book designer himself (proprietor of the Greenwood Press in San Francisco), Jack Stauffacher continues this line of craftsmanship in his own books. And, although they may be rarities, they are not precious. He has always taken a practical approach to even the finest printing project, making books that are meant to be read, not just admired.

It goes on
Sumner Stone's interview with Jack Stauffacher, the concurrent exhibit at the San Francisco Center for the Book of Stauffacher's work, the presence of Hermann and Gudrun Zapf at both, and the existence of Zapfest itself — these all draw the threads tight between old tradi-tions and contemporary craft. The art of communication that we practice today is based firmly in techniques and intellectual habits that go back hundreds of years. And it's the connections made, and the opportunities created, by individual people in their everyday work that make it all possible.

INDEX